Reaching and Teaching Young Adolescents

Gloria Goris Stronks
Nancy Knol

Succeeding in Deeper Waters

Reaching and Teaching Young Adolescents

www.acsi.org
All Rights Reserved
Association of Christian Schools International
Colorado Springs, Colorado

No portion of this book may be reproduced in any way without the written permission of ACSI and the author, except for brief excerpts in reviews by magazines or professional journals.

Reaching and Teaching Young Adolescents:
Succeeding in Deeper Waters
© 1999 Gloria Goris Stronks and Nancy Knol
Editor: Mary Endres
Designer: DAScott

Printed in the United States of America
ISBN 1-58331-024-x

This book is dedicated to Mike, and Phep, and Adam . . .
who all taught their teachers
while
they were here with us on earth.

It all begins with relationship

Reaching and Teaching Young Adolescents

Contents

Introduction vii

Chapter 1:   The Middle School Years 1

Chapter 2:   Great Expectations, Great Challenges 15

Chapter 3:   Growing Accustomed to the Dark 33

Chapter 4:   Finding a Way Through 49

Chapter 5:   What Are We Supposed to Teach? 63

Chapter 6:   Finding Your Word in the Gospels 81

Chapter 7:   Teaching Responsive Discipleship 95

Chapter 8:   "Panting, He Purchased the Pearl" 107

Appendix: Ideas from the Field 117

Reaching and Teaching Young Adolescents

Introduction

"What exactly is it that you students wanted to have happen in grades seven and eight?" A moment of silence followed the outburst of the frustrated principal. Then one of the eleventh-grade boys answered. "Respect! We wanted to be respected by our teachers and parents!" And the eight other eleventh graders nodded in agreement.

It was the opening day of a one-week workshop for Christian middle school teachers and principals. The setting couldn't have been lovelier, a Salvation Army camp in the hills above Manly, just north of Sydney, Australia. From the deck where morning tea had been served, we could see the ocean just below. Beautiful green and yellow birds sat on the railing of the deck, watching for crumbs. Nine eleventh-grade students from the local Christian secondary school had been selected by their principal because they had successfully completed grades seven and eight, and had gone on to become competent, articulate high school students. These young people took their seats on the platform, looking wonderfully poised in their attractive school uniforms. The sixty-five middle school teachers and principals, from all parts of Australia, were invited to ask questions about what these young people remembered of their experiences in grades seven and eight.

The moderator began with the first question: "What do you remember learning in grades seven and eight?" The silence that followed was deafening until a girl said, "If you mean what do we remember learning about academic matters, I'm sorry, but I remember nothing at all that I learned then." When asked how that was possible, she continued, "You see, we passed tests and did our assignments and made satisfactory grades, but nothing we were taught was at all relevant to our lives at that point." The rest of the students chimed in, supporting her observation. Questions from the floor came at a rapid pace.

The students were poised but firm in their agreement that it is possible to do satisfactory work, even outstanding academic work, in a traditional seventh- or eighth-grade setting and still not be learning. The educators leaned forward, trying to understand what it was these young people meant when they said that what they were taught should have been more closely related to their life experiences. Finally had come the question, "What is it that you students *wanted* to have happen?" The answer—"Respect!"—came from a boy who, until that moment, had said nothing at all. He added, "And we wanted to have *earned* that respect."

Every student on that platform backed him in his claim that <u>seventh and eighth graders want to be respected more than anything else. And they want that respect to include respecting the knowledge and life experiences they have already gained as well as personal respect for them as people</u>. Australian Christian middle schoolers are not the only ones who would ask for respect. North American students might word the answer differently, but their meaning would be the same.

No area of Christian schooling has changed so dramatically in the last decade as that which we've come to call "middle school." The changes have resulted from new information about how twelve-to-fourteen-year-old students think and learn. We know more about the physical and emotional development of young adolescents than we did, and we know far more about the way they learn. They have made it clear that they want and need our respect, but also that they want to know they have earned it.

<u>The most important goal of the Christian middle school is that students will learn to be and act like disciples of Jesus Christ</u>. Pastors, Christian parents, and teachers often assume that if children study the Bible they will be responsive disciples

Introduction

when they are adults. Unfortunately that assumption isn't true. Discipleship is learned the same way we learn many other things, by doing. And it is in doing acts of discipleship—learning about various kinds of work, helping those who need help, taking responsibility for the classroom climate—that middle school students will come to feel the respect they are asking for. They will know that they are respected, and they will respect themselves.

In the following pages we are not going to say much about what middle school students are like or why they need a particular kind of schooling. Most teachers and principals working at this level already understand those things. Rather, we will address issues that were not part of the book *The Christian Middle School: An Ethos of Caring* (1990). Chapter 1 explains why Christian middle schools are needed so much at the present time. Chapter 2 presents research findings about how girls and boys in state-supported schools act toward each other as well as the results of our study about how middle school students in Christian schools act toward each other, with suggestions for how we might improve. Middle school teachers are often faced with the grief students feel over the illness or death of someone dear to them, and chapter 3 addresses that pain. Chapter 4 explains what works in middle school in light of how students at that level learn. Chapter 5 addresses the subject of designing curriculum, and chapter 6 describes one approach to teaching eighth-grade Bible. In chapter 7 we deal with the issue of assessment. Many teachers have asked for ideas concerning devotions and worship in middle school, and we respond in chapter 8. We sent out a request to middle school teachers for ideas that work in their schools. You'll find some of those ideas in chapter 5, and we'll include others in the Appendix.

The two of us have somewhat different writing styles, perhaps in part because our daily tasks differ. One of us has taught for a number of years but is presently a college faculty member doing research on middle school students. The other has been a teacher of middle school students for ten years. For that reason we have identified the writer of each chapter. We hope our separate voices will provide a refreshing contrast.

Throughout the book, student comments will be set off with appropriate type. The illustrations within were drawn by eighth-grade students. We are enormously grateful for the students who contributed their writing and drawings, to those who responded to the surveys, to those teachers who distributed and collected the survey results, and to those who contributed their own ideas for what works in Christian middle schools.

Chapter 1

The Middle School Years
Have Dreams and Heroes Died?

I recently returned from a family gathering in central Minnesota, the place of my childhood. The drive past the fields of black earth and varying shades of green plants filled me with the nostalgia typical of most of us when we visit our past. As I drove, I thought how different the colors around me were from those I had seen just two weeks earlier in central Australia. The colors of these fields were in strong contrast to Australia's red earth and soft shades of blue-green foliage, even though both lie under the widest of skies. Surely the Master Artist is at work in many ways.

That same hand has created all the girls and boys we see in our schools, revealing the many ways it is possible to reflect God's image. We sometimes think the task of the Christian school is to teach students to conform to a model that reflects our own narrow understanding rather than the diverse ways God's image can be reflected. At no level is this misunderstanding more evident than in grades seven and eight. That is because our traditional attitudes have risen out of a belief that our most important tasks are to help seventh and eighth graders through the "problems of adolescence" so they will conform to societal norms, and to "get them ready for secondary school." Now we recognize that our real task is to help middle school students gain understandings that are developmentally appropriate for their level—to know God's wonderful created world and to find their own place in that world.

Someone asked us recently, "Given all the literature on school reform, why do you focus on middle school kids?" Our answer was that because of the complexities of modern society, middle schoolers are the most vulnerable children in school today. During this time of great vulnerability, middle school students frequently face a less nurturing and supportive environment than ever before. In fact, some school reform measures actually encourage a *less* supportive environment for middle schoolers. We must be careful because what happens to them at this level determines to a great extent their future success or failure.

When we say they are vulnerable, we are talking not only about at-risk students in danger of dropping out of school. All middle school children experience enormous physical and emotional changes at a time when society sends them messages along these lines: *It's important to fit in*, *Compete so you'll be the best*, and *Try to act and look like a high school student*. Pressures to conform to such societal norms are very real and are especially troublesome because middle schoolers' physical development doesn't follow a neat pattern. Some may grow from six to twelve inches and gain twenty to forty pounds in these years, while others don't begin their adolescent growth until well into high school. Bodies change in shape, agility, and strength, while complexions suffer.

What is unusual about this? In themselves, the changes are normal, but they are happening earlier than ever. For various reasons, both positive and negative, early adolescence now encompasses the greatest pubertal change of any time in human history. For the grandparents and great-grandparents of these students, such changes didn't happen until late in their high school years.

Young adolescents of earlier generations knew they were needed. Their help was wanted, if not for the family to survive, at least for things to work smoothly. Knowing they were needed and responding to that need deepened the maturity of earlier twelve-to-fourteen-year-olds. Are our young people truly needed? Today's middle school students have the emotions that accompany the onset of puberty along with the lack of maturity caused by decreased societal and parental needs and expectations. The situation is extremely confusing for them.

Dreams and Heroes

Young people of earlier times found direction for the future by looking around them for adults who were living meaningful lives. In a real sense those adults became their heroes, and not only nearby adults but well-known public figures.

Heroes are often people who can do splendid things or provide respected leadership in the home, church, school, and larger society because they live meaningful lives. I'm afraid that today's society makes it extremely difficult for adolescents to find such heroes. Those who look to their parents for role models are frequently disappointed, and it's difficult for young people whose attitudes are shaped by television to identify national heroes to provide them with direction. Heroes of earlier times—Presidents Jefferson, Lincoln, F. D. Roosevelt, Eisenhower—might have fared quite differently in the eyes of young people if their lives and actions had been scrutinized closely and referred to disparagingly on a powerful medium like television. The same is true of earlier sports heroes. Exemplary role models are hard to find among today's leaders, in part because television has brought their serious flaws into sharp focus.

With few heroes, it is increasingly difficult for young people to have a vision . . . one that can give them hope and direction to the future, a vision that says, *If you go this way, you'll be on the right track and will live a worthwhile Christian life.* Without such a vision, our young people's souls are in jeopardy.

Along with the influence of television, there is the overwhelming me-ism in North American society. An almost single-minded concern with self, *what's going to happen to me*, and with material things grows out of fear, lack of trust, and a generalized cynicism. Most ten-to-twelve-year-olds are idealistic. They think all kinds of things are possible. As they grow older, they lose their trust of people they trusted and learn to fear the world around them, so their earlier idealism is replaced by cynicism. They come to believe that what they think doesn't count for much, that the people running the country don't care what happens to them, that public leaders don't know what they are doing, and that the rich get richer and the poor get poorer. Cynical people are unable to believe that reform activities will do any good at all, so they find it difficult to work toward reclaiming any part of the world for Jesus Christ. There's a real danger that our children are growing up without a vision at a time when they most need one.

Helping Students Find a Vision
What is a vision for young people between twelve and fourteen?

For Christians a vision ought to be founded on the Word of God. As children grow up, they also need to be able to look at adult Christians who are leading lives they admire, doing things they respect . . . adults whose lives are whole and exemplary. We find that children as young as twelve and thirteen who have a close relationship with an adult doing admirable work and living a life of wholeness do better work in middle school, and their stronger achievement continues through high school. Children fare better when they have an example of someone they want to be like. That's why we want middle school students to know adult Christians who live exemplary lives, and to see adults in a broad range of work experiences.

A Christian adult may inspire a vision, but that vision will remain only a dream unless the student gets to know the adult as a mentor. Then, as the mentor shares—*Here is how this all comes about. . . . This is what you might have to go through. . . . This is why I make the decisions I do*—the young adolescent will come to understand the tasks that go with the vision. Without a vision, the tasks young people must do become drudgery. Unless they hear about the tasks, the vision remains nothing but a dream.

Some middle and high school young people are excellent students, and we have high hopes for them as future leaders.

Chapter 1

And some have great difficulty with learning, and we try to provide the necessary support. But in between we have a large group of what some have called "unspecial" students. They do their schoolwork grudgingly. Some of them like being with their middle school friends but view studying as wholly unrelated to real life. Again, a task without a vision is drudgery.

Because our world has become so complicated, all young people—scholars, strugglers, "unspecial"—need to see their parents, teachers, ministers, and other adults of their faith community as people who live with vision. They need to share in our vision and understand the tasks that go with it. They need all that, for much will be expected of them in this increasingly strange and difficult world.

What is a discipleship curriculum for middle school?

The curriculum of any Christian middle school should enable students to explore God's creation, to discern the effects of sin on the world, and to understand themselves so that they can develop responses to Christ's reconciling work and become equipped to serve Him in all of life. This is what we are called to do as disciples of Jesus Christ, and so, in a very real sense, the Christian school curriculum can be called a *discipleship* curriculum.

What might a discipleship curriculum include?

It has three parts. First, research supports the notion that those middle school students who leave eighth grade with some idea of a career in which they might use their gifts are much more successful in high school and college or technical school. Therefore, a discipleship curriculum should ensure that students learn the responsibilities involved in various kinds of work. Students must learn to look at themselves and understand areas of God's world where their gifts could be used. Perhaps it's time we remove exploratory units from the Christian middle school curriculum and make certain that every unit we teach has a strong component about kinds of work God's people do in that arena. For example, in a unit on justice the students visit a courtroom when cases are being heard and talk with or help people whose jobs have to do with the law: attorney, judge,

Reaching and Teaching Young Adolescents

court recorder, police officer, social worker, and many others. In a unit on wellness they might go into a hospital or clinic and talk with or help people who are caring for those who are ill or helping those who are well stay well. In a unit on community they might visit community centers to talk with or help people who are supporting those in need. In a unit on marshlands they might meet with or help an environmentalist working to preserve the wetlands and find out what jobs are available in environmental work. I am not suggesting that schools have a week in which each student "shadows" or helps an adult in the workplace. My suggestion is that we plan our units carefully so that students will be far better informed than they presently are concerning what kinds of work God's people do and what difficult issues they may face in that work.

Second, a discipleship curriculum should take seriously the idea that, in an affluent society, a middle school curriculum must include <u>opportunities for students to help those in need</u>. Sixth and seventh graders might help students in the lower elementary school who are having difficulty with reading or math. Together the older and younger students might write and publish books or do art work. On school time one afternoon each week, eighth graders might talk with and read to elderly people in a rest home or help in a food kitchen or work in a day care center. They might have a partnership with a student in an inner city school, going there one afternoon a week to read with their younger "buddy." Such experiences would be integrated into their middle school curriculum in ways that would help them understand the needs of others and consider how they might help to meet those needs.

Third, a discipleship curriculum would mean that middle school students would <u>understand their responsibilities to each other.</u> To that end, teachers could use strategies like those listed by Evelyn Schneider in the article "Giving Students a Voice in the Classroom" (*Educational Leadership,* September, 1996, pp. 22-26). Strategies such as setting up conflict negotiation in the classroom, designing creative restitutions and logical consequences, and having class meetings concerning the classroom community are effective in helping students understand how their actions affect others.

Of course, a middle grade discipleship curriculum will include the knowledge and skills we believe are appropriate for those grades, but the content must always be related closely to students' lives. And interwoven through this part of the curriculum will be the three aspects of discipleship just described.

Developmental Needs of Middle Schoolers *Imp.*

When we plan the middle school curriculum, we will want to keep in mind the particular developmental needs of students of that age:

1. Every middle school student wants to believe in herself. If she feels unsuccessful, very often she will stop trying. She has to in order to save face. After all, if I try and fail, I am ashamed. But if I don't try and then fail, I don't have to be ashamed because I know I would have been successful if I *had* tried. Every middle school student needs to feel success as a person.
2. Every middle school student wants to be liked and respected. He wants to be respected by his peers, teachers, and parents, even when he acts as if he doesn't care.
3. Every middle school student needs physical exercise and freedom to move around. Without exercise and movement his rapidly growing body will hurt.
4. Every middle school student wants life to be just. He doesn't always treat his peers with justice, but he needs to learn to do so. And he can't flourish if he sees injustice around him, even though he will not always come to the defense of another who is treated unjustly.
5. Every middle school student spends time thinking about what will happen to her in the future. As already noted, students who have some idea of an area of life that might provide them with a career will be more successful in high school and beyond.

An Excellent Christian Middle School

Parker Palmer says that Christian teachers ought to be "making a space for learning in which obedience to Truth may be practiced." If that is true, then the space for learning in a Christian middle school must have the following characteristics:

1. The school must help students recognize and unwrap the gifts God has given to them. These gifts are of many kinds, and students in a Christian middle school must learn to expect others to be different and to celebrate their own God-created differences. Therefore, each student must be guided to reflect carefully on his personal strengths and weaknesses and to take personal responsibility for his own development.

2. The school's teaching will lead students to ask and answer foundational questions, such as, *When God created this part of the world, what do you believe His intentions were? Is this part of creation the way God intended it to be? If it is broken, what went wrong? What should we be doing to bring this part of creation back to the way God wants it to be?*

3. Students share each other's joys and bear each other's burdens. Each student learns to take responsibility for the learning, care, and nurture of others. No matter how successful one student is, there really is no success unless other students are succeeding and feel successful at developing their own gifts. All of us rejoice over the successes of each one as we do over our own, and all of us grieve over each other's burdens as we grieve over our own.

4. The entire climate is one of seeking God's shalom. A Christian school is a community—God's community—and one's actions toward others in the classroom, in the halls, in the teachers' lounge, and on the playground are what form that community. The little actions of each day really do matter a great deal.

5. All learning is planned to be in keeping with how students learn and develop at different age levels. Teachers do not view learning as "stuffing knowledge into students' heads" but rather as an ongoing spiral. In this learning spiral, students encounter something new, think they know and understand it, work or play with it, reflect on it, and finally say, "Oh, *now* I get it"—the *"aha* moment." Middle school teachers must recognize that such a moment will be different for each student, and they must plan with the students a learning space filled with varied learning activities to move each student toward that moment.

It is neither new nor unique for Christian middle school teachers to make heartfelt commitments to helping their students learn responsive discipleship. Therefore, many of the characteristics described here exist to some extent in many classrooms. But what is happening today with the Christian middle school movement is that entire school communities—teachers, staff, parents, and students—commit themselves to working toward the common goal of learning and living in responsive discipleship and sharing openly with each other while doing so.

A school doesn't adopt this way of learning overnight, nor even in a year or two. Teachers involved in Christian middle schools continue to need a great deal of support in the form of in-service training even when they are well into the new plan. They will continue to need team planning time in addition to their personal planning time. Parents will need careful and regular communication so that they can support the school and take an active role in their children's education. Above all, the middle school students themselves must be involved in the planning so that they view the curriculum as personally relevant.

Christian middle schools that have made significant changes in recent years can be found in regions as far apart and as dissimilar as California, Michigan, Florida, and New Mexico;

British Columbia and Ontario in Canada; Darwin in the Northern Territory of Australia and Melbourne at the southern point. In each case, the changes did not originate with a school board member or an administrator. Rather, one or two teachers began talking about the reading they were doing on what is happening in middle schools. As more teachers became interested, a leadership team was appointed, often consisting of the principal and two or three teachers, along with a parent-board member, to select readings around which staff discussions would center.

One of the first steps was to examine the school's current mission statement to see whether it reflected insights gained from reading about what works in educating young adolescents. In most cases they discovered that the mission statement needed to be revised to reflect new understandings of development and learning at this level. In spite of initial reluctance to spend time in this reflection rather than move immediately toward change, this reexamination of the mission statement has consistently provided opportunities for serious dialogue that has been surprisingly profitable and important for planning appropriate Christian schooling for the coming decade.

The next step was to examine the entire school program in light of the newly revised mission statement to see what needed changing. Once the needed changes were agreed on, a chronology or sequence of events was planned. Too many changes at the same time can quickly lead to confusion and a loss of teacher morale.

Although the teachers in the different schools have read many of the same books and articles, the changes have not made these schools look exactly alike. Schooling must reflect not only a particular philosophy, recent research, and state or provincial requirements, but also the needs of a given community and the rich gifts and experiences of its teachers, students, and parents.

Chapter 1

In Praise of the Strenuous Life

The following project was used in a freshmen ori[entation] course by Mark Davis, high school principal at Cha[ttanooga] Christian School in Tennessee, but it could be used with eight graders as well. The project is called "In Praise of the Strenuous Life," and its purpose is to use 1 Peter 1:13 to challenge students to a life of self-control and sensitize them to a deeper life in Christ. Davis begins the course by reading aloud a speech by Theodore Roosevelt entitled "In Praise of the Strenuous Life." He then challenges the students to do the following for one week:

- You will not listen to or watch anything on the radio, television, stereo, the theater, or the computer. In other words, you must pull the plug for one week.
- You will complete every homework assignment, striving for an A grade on each.
- You will study for tests and complete all projects, striving for an A grade.
- Each day you will rise exactly one hour earlier than usual. In this hour, you will find a place of solitude, where you will meditate on the Lord. You will also retire one hour earlier than usual. In this hour you will read anything of your choosing for thirty minutes and write in your journal for the remaining thirty minutes. You'll close your day in prayer.
- You will remain after school Tuesday through Friday and the following Monday to run/walk for a continuous thirty minutes (from 3:30 to 4:00). You will follow the same routine on Saturday on your own.
- You will interview someone over seventy years old and ask the person to tell his life story. You will write out the details (use a tape recorder if you must) of the person's story and give him/her a copy of it. Suggested questions include: When and where were you born? What did your parents do for a living? Did you have siblings? What was school like for you? What are your memories of your growing-up years? What were some of the most joyful times of your youth?

Reaching and Teaching Young Adolescents

What were some of the hardest? What was your courtship like? Tell me about your spouse. What jobs have you held? What are your hobbies? Did you have children? What joys and sorrows have you faced in your adult life? Where do you find peace and joy? What is your belief in God? Compare your life today with your life as it used to be.
- You will choose one evening to rise at 3:00 A.M. and pray for thirty minutes.

In addition, Davis also uses recommended exercises based on the book *Space for God* by Don Postema (Grand Rapids, MI: CRC Publications, 1985).

Model Christian Middle Schools

Recently I attended a Christian school regional conference and spoke with teachers and principals of middle schools that were at various points in carrying out their plans for change. We were having a "cracker barrel" session in which groups from each school described what was happening in their school. I heard so much that was happening in each school that finally I asked, "Are any of you exhausted from all the planning and changing at your school?" They all chuckled and admitted that they were often tired but never sorry they were making the change because they were convinced that the new way of doing Christian schooling did far more to help their students learn responsive discipleship. I asked whether they ever suffered from a lack of ideas for better ways of carrying out their plans. They agreed they'd been blessed with too many ideas so that now and then they had to place any new one into an "idea bank" to be drawn from only when they had all the present activities well in hand.

"You've been developing your middle schools for a number of years now," I went on. "Surely some of you can say that you have a finished product and are now somewhat of a model for others interested in this kind of schooling?" There was no immediate answer, but I could hear the undercurrent of mur-

Chapter 1

mured disagreement. Then one principal stood up and seemed to speak for everyone.

"You may invite others to our school, and we'll try to show them what we are doing and tell them how we came to this point. But you may never, ever, call us a 'model Christian middle school.' We're pleased and grateful for what is happening in our school, but I doubt whether we'll ever reach our goal."

It is possible that developing a Christian middle school is much like the learning of our middle school students—a process, with our learning always in progress. Like our students, we reach our "*aha* moments" time after time. You might be surprised to hear us say of a particular part of our program, "Oh, *now* I get it"—knowing that as long as we teach we will "get it" over and over. Christian middle schools are exciting, vibrant places these days, and they truly are "spaces for learning in which obedience to Truth may be practiced."

For Discussion

1. As a group of teachers, predict who the heroes of your middle school students are. Then ask each student to write a paragraph about his or her hero. How do the results compare?
2. Which elements of a discipleship curriculum are the strongest in your middle school? Which elements need strengthening?

Chapter 2

Great Expectations, Great Challenges
Is This How Middle School Students Are Supposed to Act?

Middle school is a pivotal stage for all students. What happens or doesn't happen to them during those years has far-reaching effects. The *Middle School Initiative*, a study funded by the Kellogg Foundation, emphasizes that the middle school years are a "time of risk and challenge," and that successful middle school experiences are critical to students' later achievement. The report reveals that students of middle school age are full of high expectations, but they face many risks. They are children one moment and adults the next. Their suicide rate is increasing. While the pregnancy rate among high school girls is dropping, it is steadily rising among middle school girls, as is addictive behavior, such as smoking and using alcohol and drugs. The latter is particularly frightening because we know that addictive behavior is much more difficult to change when it is begun early.

Does belonging to a school community of people who claim membership in the family of Christ help middle schoolers through this tumultuous time? We believe and trust that it does. Even so, teachers and parents must realize the fragility of these years and must strengthen the institutions that have the greatest influence on their young adolescents: the home, the school, and the larger faith community. Our emphasis in this chapter is on strengthening the Christian middle school so that it will provide much-needed support for its students.

Perhaps we will be helped most by remembering ourselves at their age. Do you remember a time when walking across the front of the auditorium was almost more than you could bear? When, after joining a group at lunch, you suddenly realized they

Reaching and Teaching Young Adolescents

didn't really want you there? When some members of your class regularly picked on one student and called him names, and you sat quietly by, not daring to take his part? When you would lie in bed at night, trying desperately to plan how you might combine your few sweaters and slacks so your classmates wouldn't suspect how meager your wardrobe was?

Until recently, almost all research on middle school students was based on the assumption that girls and boys experience school the same way. It wasn't until the landmark 1991 publication of *The AAUW Report: How Schools Shortchange Girls* that recommendations about schooling took gender into account. That report and others like it demonstrated that girls' self-esteem and confidence in their own academic competence drop precipitously during the middle school years, narrowing their choices of course work and career path. According to this research, teachers give more classroom attention and more esteem-building encouragement to boys than to girls. Teachers tend to select instructional materials that interest boys, on the assumption that if we can interest the boys the class will go well because the girls will follow. Also, teachers often stereotype boys and girls according to ability—mathematical, spatial, even verbal—in ways that are not supported by research (Stronks and Blomberg, 1993).

A more recent publication, *Girls in the Middle: Working to Succeed in School* (AAUW, 1996), reports that in thousands of classrooms, well-meaning teachers continue to deliver subtle but powerful messages reinforcing boys' dominance in the classroom and in life. The girls' dilemma is presented as follows:

> Adolescent girls struggle with an often contradictory set of expectations. They are to be sexy and flirtatious but at the same time remain "good girls." They are to fend off aggressive male attention while simultaneously meeting their teachers' expectations of nonaggressive behavior. Females are to put domestic life first at the same time that they prepare for financial independence. (p. 2)

Chapter 2

What About Boys?

Are boys, then, in a favored situation in school? Hardly! They face restrictive gender stereotypes of their own. They are pressured to be tough rather than vulnerable, but those who are too tough may be branded troublemakers. They receive the message from their peers that it isn't cool for boys to be interested in academics. When the more studious boys see their teachers joke and banter with boys who think learning is unimportant, they tend to think the teacher views those less studious boys as more interesting. Their self-esteem is weakened, and it seems to some almost as if the teachers are part of the plot against them.

> *I just hated my Christian elementary school. In fact I disliked school all the way through grade eight. I really liked learning things, and to be so interested was just simply uncool in my school . . . especially for a guy. Even the teachers seemed to think it was uncool. At least they always joked around with the other boys who weren't into the school thing as much as I was. But the last two high school years were a lot better for me. There I had teachers who really respected that I wanted to learn. And college is great.*
> —Senior male student at Calvin College

The fact is that very little is known or has been studied about how school practices encourage or inhibit boys (Cushner et al., 1992).

Teachers will want to think about what is happening in their classrooms right now. Which of the following practices, identified by Gary D. Borich and Martin Tombari (1997), do we find in our own classrooms?

- Teachers use feminine pronouns in referring to a teacher, nurse, or social worker but masculine pronouns for an engineer, doctor, or lawyer.
- Teachers more often call on boys in math or science, and on girls in language arts.
- Girls and boys are grouped during recess for activities that reflect sex-role biases.

Reaching and Teaching Young Adolescents

- Teachers and counselors give different career advice to girls than to boys.
- Teachers address boys from across the classroom but girls from arm's length or less.
- Teachers reprimand boys more sharply and more often than girls for the same behavior.
- Teachers praise girls for choosing activities associated with traditional gender roles.
- Female teachers express in students' hearing their distaste for, and inability to do, math.
- Teachers correct boys for academic mistakes but refrain from doing the same with girls.
- Teachers consistently call on boys more often than girls. (p. 524)

A Survey of Middle School Students in Christian Schools

Recently a survey was conducted with sixth, seventh, and eighth grade students in seventeen schools belonging to Christian Schools International (CSI) and representing various regions in North America. Students were asked to respond to the following questions concerning relationships in their schools:

1. Do all the students in your grade seem to get along well with each other, or do some students appear to lack friends and to be left out of things?
2. When I was a student in your grade, some of the boys talked to some girls in mean ways that were hurtful and went way beyond teasing. In fact, they called those girls names, and the rest of us didn't dare tell the boys they were wrong because we were afraid we'd be next on their list. These girls never dared to tell their parents or teachers, but they felt miserable about it. Does that happen in your school? If so, describe what you mean.
3. In your class who answers questions and participates more, boys or girls, or do boys and girls participate

Chapter 2

    about the same? If it is not the same, why do you think that is true?
4. If you were the teacher in your class and yet could still see everything from the students' point of view, what would you do to make all the students feel comfortable, secure, and worthwhile?

Of a total of 1314 responses, 223 students said boys answer more questions and participate more often than girls, and 287 students said the same of girls; 804 students said girls and boys respond about the same amount. Those numbers sound fairly well balanced. However, students in any given class were much in agreement on whether girls or boys participate more frequently in class discussion.

In classes in which girls participated more frequently, the reason given by both girls and boys was that in their school it is not cool for a boy to show that he cares about studying or knowing things. The sad fact is that in some Christian schools the culture is such that boys will be teased mercilessly if they do well in school.

The boys want to feel cool and look cool so they don't answer much. If we do, it's like, "yes," or "no."

A guy usually wants to act cool, and he doesn't want to make his friends think he's a geek so he doesn't answer questions.

I think that girls seem to care more about their school work and that for guys, we think that it's not cool to be smart and know a lot, so the boys do not raise their hand as much as the girls do. In math, which has a male teacher, the boys participate more.

For us boys, doing well in school just isn't macho.

In classes in which boys participated more frequently, the reason given by most students was that girls aren't as smart as boys, or girls are shy and would rather gossip and talk about how they look than think about what they are studying.

Girls often gave this reason:
The girls are intimidated by the boys. They mock us if we don't participate, but if we do they mock us for that too.

One boy explained it this way:
Boys raise their hand before they know the answer. Girls wait until they know the answer.

One girl agreed:
Us girls don't want to make fools of ourselves if we're wrong.

Fortunately, there are classes in which almost all students report that girls and boys respond to the same extent. Answers such as the following were frequent:
Our class is very good at discussions when we get going.

I think in our class no one is afraid to participate and no one feels stupid. None of us feel that we'll be made fun of if we respond. Usually no one makes fun or ridicules unless they are just teasing.

An important goal of teaching is to involve all students, girls and boys, in taking responsibility for their own learning and for helping each other learn, as well. A teaching staff will want to examine carefully the culture of their own classrooms and of the whole school, asking, "Are the conditions in this school as good as they possibly can be for involving each student in learning?" If the teachers discover that their school's culture is such that boys cannot allow themselves to be involved in learning because they won't be cool or that girls aren't participating for their own reasons, the issue must be openly addressed in a meeting with students and their parents. The basic task of the Christian school is to enable each student to be all that God intends that

Chapter 2

student to be. The harmful elements of our culture *can* be overcome.

When it comes to student relationships, a large majority of the students spoke very positively, saying that most students get along well and are kind to each other. However, after reading a few responses like the following, one gets a hint that in many classes there's more to the story:

> *There are still some kids left out of things. Even though we may go to a Christian school, not everyone acts as a Christian should. I know I don't either, though.*

> *Yes, because sometimes there's a standard that the cool kids have, and some people just don't meet their standards and are left out.*

> *There are some students who don't have friends. At recess they sort of walk around by themselves. Most of us get along, though. We're kind of like one big happy family. Some people who are, I guess, immature, hang out with people in younger grades. I feel bad for people who don't have any friends.*

> *All the students in my school get along. I am one of a few students who doesn't have friends. People pick on me a lot. They care what's on the outside . . . not the inside. It makes me feel bad to see people be hurt by other people because I know how it feels. It's not very fun!!*

In her book *School Talk: Gender and Adolescent Culture* (1995), Donna Eder describes the results of a research project concerning student-student interactions and student-staff interactions at Woodview School, a large public middle school in the Midwest. The team of four researchers spent from five to twelve months observing lunchroom, restroom, and hallway interactions and conversations.

Remembering the findings of James Coleman (1961) revealing the pervasive adolescent concern for popularity over academic success, Eder was not surprised when her team encountered similar attitudes. Other studies (Cusick, 1973; Eckert, 1989) have shown the same link between participation in extracurricular activities and peer status. According to her research, this preoccupation is due in part to the strong role that extracurricular activities have historically played in American high schools (p. 13). What appears to happen is that students who participate in key extracurricular activities, such as boys' athletics and girls' cheerleading, have greater visibility, and visibility is key to being known by many students. Extracurricular activities also allow students to have greater control of their time.

Middle schools offer fewer extracurricular activities than high schools, often just boys' basketball and girls' cheerleading. Musical electives, such as choir and band, do not appear to give students much visibility among their peers. The absence of other opportunities for gaining visibility may lead to the cliques and rankings that are present in many middle schools. Roberta Simmons and Dale Blyth (1987) report that students who attend traditional junior high schools have much lower self-esteem throughout junior and senior high than do students whose seventh and eighth grades are part of a K-8 system. Schools that have made serious efforts to incorporate elements of the middle school concept are finding ways to overcome the problems caused by selective visibility.

Cliques, Rankings, and Name-Calling

Are there cliques and rankings in Christian schools? Student reports concerning any specific school tend to be consistent. In other words, if there are cliques and rankings, every student knows it; and if there aren't, they know that too. In two classes of the seventeen schools, almost all of the students said something like the following:

Chapter 2

> *Most people in my class do get along well. We all play games. We do not exclude anyone. At lunch and at parties, everyone is together.*

That was not the case in other classes or in most schools, however. Even students who had found their own place in the system knew that ranking was happening and that some classmates were being hurt by it.

> *There are a couple of different levels of people in my school. Some are stuck-up and consider themselves to be the most popular. Lots of kids are treated differently though, especially if they are different looking or are friends with people that aren't so cool.*

> *In our school we seem to have our own little groups that are friends. Some are nice, some are stupid gang bangers, some are big, some are small. And some people are alone.*

> *I think that there are people who get left out a lot. I know that people don't leave them out on purpose. It's just that those people don't try to include themselves. People do try to include those who are alone, but if those people just sit there and expect you to invite them, it's not going to work. I will invite people to hang out, but if they don't try to be a part there is no sense in me trying. Because I, personally, don't like to be around shy people.*

In the Woodview Middle School study (1995), Eder describes the ranking system among the students. She says it came about largely because the school provided opportunities for certain students to have more visibility than others through participation in such elite activities as cheerleading, football, and basketball. Ranking was particularly strong in school whose athletic teams played against teams from other schools. The absence of any distinct popular groups in the sixth grade, where these activities were not offered, supports her view. Visibility is central to a student's popularity because many other students know and talk to one who is highly visible.

In Christian schools, students often spoke of a three-level ranking system, with the groups usually being defined by money and appearance. The students' insights concerning how the ranking system worked were uncanny:

> *There are some kids who lack friends, but most of the people get along pretty well. There is the very popular group and the people who are kind of popular but not always invited to the parties. And there are the people who don't get invited to parties and get made fun of.*

> *We seem to have three groups: the popular, the normal, and the unpopular. The popular group contains the most friends, and everyone has everything, including looks. The normal are everyday kids who have quite a few friends. The unpopular seem to be those who don't have a lot of money and are quiet and keep to themselves. It's sad that they don't have many friends.*

> *Well, we have three groups; the cool group, the okay group, and the losers group. The cool group always makes fun of the two other groups, and lots of people in the cool group get in fights with other people in the cool group. The okay group makes fun of the losers group. They don't have very many fights. Lots of people in that group have best friends. The losers group always gets made fun of. They are all best friends and have some problems in school academically. The losers group has the fewest people in it.*

A number of students revealed their own uneasiness about the ranking system. They seemed to be completely aware that classmates were being hurt by it:

> *Well, some of the students that act immature are sometimes mocked or left out. Even so, at the risk of being mocked, a few students, like me, try their best to include the excluded.*

Chapter 2

> *I feel that as a whole, the grade seems to get along, although there are a few people who get harassed and left out when something important comes along. The students who seem to lack in social acceptance only have friends that are true and genuine, and that are willing to risk their reputation to help somebody who needs help—who is being nailed down so hard it is hard to get out. In times of hardship and despair we all seem to come together, however. We are bound with our Christian love and no longer place labels of "popular" and "outcast." We seem to be one and help one another get through the bad situation. The outcasts are too often left out and lack in friends. Then somebody gets an opinion about an outcast, and it sticks and everybody agrees. We don't get to the point where I could say that one student was evil and cruel to another, but it is pretty close.*

Along with ranking goes name-calling, according to Eder and others. Thorne and Luria (1986) reported that, as early as elementary school, boys are using sexual insults and approaching male-female relations in a daring, aggressive manner. The insults made to girls usually carried negative sexual labels, such as "slut" and "slag." Canaan (1991) found that high-status boys often verbally insulted and physically harassed low-status, often overweight boys.

In the Christian school study, a similar scenario was described in which boys talked to girls in mean and hurtful ways that went far beyond teasing. The students were asked if that ever occurred in their school. A large majority of students said that it never would and that if it did, they themselves would step in and correct it. But in eighty-five percent of the schools, one or two students said they know it happens because it happens to them. A very few said it was just the other way around, with the girls saying mean and hurtful things to the boys. Some suggested that it happens more to new students who have just transferred in. In most cases, this name-calling is not done by all, or even most, of the students. Nevertheless, it is clear that in many schools, some students are being seriously hurt by other students, as these comments show:

> *It's not too bad. But sometimes boys will call girls dogs or a nerd or they go so far as to call her a bitch or something worse and diss the girls' moms. The girls never dare to tell because they think they can't really do anything about it. But I think the girls get over it pretty quick.*

> *Sometimes this one boy makes fun of me because I'm flat or because I haven't had my period yet. No, I don't tell.*

> *Yes, that kind of behavior does happen to some kids. It makes you feel that you're never good enough to do anything right. It doesn't happen very often and, if it does, it happens to the girls who don't have very many friends. Those girls need a friend to help them get through that time in their life.*

> *In our school there are really mean boys who mock girls and boys. One of my friends wants to change schools, and another was mocked at a skating party and started crying.*

> *It doesn't happen here much because most of the girls are real good friends of the guys. But if you're fat or ugly or stupid, you can get made fun of.*

> *Not many of the boys do that, but there are one or two who do that to me. They make me feel so bad that sometimes I just want to go home and cry a lot.*

> *Well, it happens but not so often. We call them names like "sluts," "whores," or "bitches."*

> *Yes, it happens here. Not a lot of people really notice because they don't pay attention. But I know that some guys always pick on some girls about stupid stuff. They do it to people who they know won't say anything. They wouldn't say it to me because I wouldn't*

Chapter 2

take it. I do sometimes say something to them if it gets too mean, but most of the time my ears go deaf to it because I hear it so often.

We have no idea whether this kind of behavior has always existed or whether it is increasing, because we have no earlier research on the subject. There has long been an attitude among parents that "boys will be boys." However, the current focus on harassment has helped teachers and parents realize that this behavior is inappropriate and must not be tolerated. If we do nothing to prevent it, we will be encouraging our young adolescents to believe that they do not have to feel responsible for another person's feelings, and that every student is out there alone.

Parents might ask why teachers don't control this behavior, but it's usually impossible for teachers to know when it happens because students don't report it. There's a fine line between reporting abusive behavior and tattling on someone who is just teasing, and the students who are being verbally abused don't know where the line is. Parents also wonder how they ought to respond when their middle school child reports such inappropriate behavior.

I told my dad, and he says boys tease girls because they like them, but that's not what this is. And so I guess I'm left to face this by myself.

In studies of 119 families, John Gottman found that parents naturally fall into two groups: those who give their children guidance about emotions and those who don't. In *The Heart of Parenting: Raising an Emotionally Intelligent Child,* he says that "the same children who in preschool are able to say, 'I don't like it when you do that,' in middle school are able to withstand normal teasing without being hurt." These children have learned how to psych out a social situation, and they have better friendships.

Reaching and Teaching Young Adolescents

But what about students who have never learned to do that, or students for whom the teasing goes beyond acceptable behavior? Are they truly left to face the pain by themselves? Is there anything that can be done about ranking and name-calling?

First, teachers and principals can make a survey of students to see whether either problem exists in their school. No national survey can tell you what you need to know about your own school. Your survey should consist of questions designed to yield that information.

Middle school students feel vulnerable and need help to feel safe about writing their true feelings, so it is wise for teachers to invite an outside person to come in and distribute the survey questions. After the teacher has left the room, the assessor should assure students of complete confidentiality and anonymity. They need not give their names. Then the students write their answers to the questions in class. No discussion should take place beforehand because others' comments would influence the students' answers. After all the surveys have been passed in, the teacher may return and lead a discussion to find out how the students perceive what is happening in their school.

Next, the teaching staff should analyze the surveys, discussing questions such as these: What is the environment like for students in our school? What steps might we take to make it an appropriate environment for young adolescents in a Christian school? It might be helpful to have an information evening for parents and students together to let them know the results of the study and the proposed improvement plans. Together, teachers, parents, and students must become aware that in Christian schools we are not simply relaxing with the comment, "Well, that's just the way young people are, you know." Instead, we are working to become more Christlike in our relationships.

Eder's study suggests that boys' insensitive and inappropriate behavior toward girls stems from a general societal focus on aggressive competition. The boys' fear of being different and of being at the bottom of the social pyramid often encourages their conformity to tough behavior. If what the studies suggest is true, ranking is a direct result of selecting a few students for more visibility and thus for more popularity. Christian schools might include intramural sports only, with every member of each team playing the same amount of time. The findings from the studies cited in this chapter suggest that an activity like cheerleading, with its focus on physical attractiveness, is not in the best interest of our girls. Instead, schools should offer sports such as track, gymnastics, volleyball, soccer, and swimming, giving girls and boys opportunities to succeed through self-competition, each competing against his other earlier scores. Parents might object, saying that life is a competition and school should ready students for life. But surely Christian schools have an obligation to prepare students for lives of responsive discipleship, lives in which they learn to help others be better at academics and athletics while at the same time working to improve their own skills.

In helping students relate more positively to each other and also to feel accepted as part of the class, a number of teachers do what this seventh-grade teacher suggests:

> Each year, after a discussion about feeling included and feeling worthwhile, I announce a writing assignment. I distribute to each student a sheet of paper with the names of all the students in the class. Their assignment is to write something that they like about each student. I do not allow any silliness or teasing comments while they are working, and on each completed paper the writer must identify him- or herself. When the assignment has been completed, I type for each student all the positive comments made by other students about her or him. There is never any indication who made which comment. I distribute the comments to the students with very little discussion.
>
> I know that this one activity has meant a great deal to students. I have had students come to me years later and tell me they still have their paper of positive comments. In fact, our local newspaper reported that a former student had his paper from middle school with him while he was away fighting in the Gulf War. That's how much the comments meant to him.

Reaching and Teaching Young Adolescents

[Care Group Info]

Both boys and girls need to have discussions concerning how sexism, and particularly a limited view of femininity and masculinity, narrows their lives. They need to understand that in some boys, athletic activities promote competitive aggressiveness that carries over into their personal relationships. They need to be alerted to the dangers that, when girls give too much attention to personal appearance, they'll see themselves as physical objects rather than the whole, complex people God intends them to be. Both boys and girls need a forum in which they can come to understand that terms such as *slut, whore,* and *bitch* keep all females locked into impossibly confining roles, and that such terms are unacceptable and will not be tolerated in the Christian school. Students need firm assurance that such language constitutes harassment and must be reported so that it can be dealt with effectively. Discussions like this could take place in advisor-advisee meetings or during homeroom. In addition, boys and girls need frequent opportunities to work together in cooperative learning, clubs, and intramural sports that emphasize playing for fun.

[Care Group Info]

While inappropriate language and actions must not be tolerated, students who seem overly sensitive to ordinary teasing need to be given better ways of dealing with it. Sometimes they are helped by learning to turn teasing into a joke on themselves. Role-playing or dramatic skits can be ways of having students practice this and other coping behaviors. Eder says that some of the most successful strategies arise from reinforcing middle schoolers' own desire to be creative and humorous as they go about the day-to-day tasks of schooling.

The students in this survey had their own ideas about how teachers might help:

> *I would tell students often that they are doing a good job. I would always be encouraging them and would let them know they could talk to me with their problems and make sure they could trust me.*

I would talk to them and get to know them and make the room kind of like their home away from home.

I would do partner activities and pair up people who usually don't hang out with each other. That way maybe they could get to know each other better and be friends.

I don't ever want anyone else to go through what I went through and to feel so miserable. I learned to come out of it, but some other kid might not. So if I were the teacher, I wouldn't ever let it happen.

If I were the teacher, I would use my favorite teacher as a role model and I would try to teach like her. I feel as if she does the job very well.

For Discussion

1. Are there cliques and rankings in your school? How can you find out? What actions might be taken on the part of teachers and parents to help students understand the harmfulness of such separation?
2. Does name-calling happen in your school? If it does, how might it be stopped? If only a very few students engage in it, how might it be stopped?
3. At what places in your curriculum is sexism discussed?
4. Do you ever discuss with your students the dangers of giving too much attention to personal appearance? What about health matters such as bulimia and anorexia?
5. How can teachers help students who are overly sensitive to ordinary teasing? What is ordinary teasing?

References

The AAUW Report: How Schools Shortchange Girls. Wellesley College Center for Research on Women, PO Box 251, Annapolis Junction, MD, 1991.

Borich, Gary D. and Martin Tombari. *Educational Psychology: A Contemporary Approach.* New York: Addison Wesley Longman, 1997.

Canaan, Joyce. "Passing Notes and Telling Jokes: Gendered Strategies Among American Middle School Teenagers," *Uncertain Terms: Negotiating Gender in American Culture.* ed. Faye Ginsburg and Anne Lowenhaupt Tsing. Boston: Beacon Press, 1991.

Cohen, Jody and Sukey Blanc. *Girls in the Middle: Working to Succeed in School.* Commissioned by the AAUW Educational Foundation, 1111 Sixteenth Street N.W. Washington, DC 20036-4873, 1996.

Coleman, James. *The Adolescent Society.* New York: Free Press, 1961.

Cushner, Kenneth, Averil McClelland, and Philip Safford. *Human Diversity in Education: An Integrative Approach.* New York: McGraw-Hill, 1992.

Cusick, Philip A. *Inside High School: The Student's World.* New York: Holt, Rinehart, and Winston, 1973.

Eckert, Penelope. *Jocks and Burnouts: Social Categories and Identity in the High School.* New York: Teachers College Press, 1989.

Eder, Donna. *School Talk: Gender and Adolescent Culture.* New Brunswick: Rutgers University Press, 1995.

Gottman, John. *The Heart of Parenting: Raising an Emotionally Intelligent Child.* Simon & Schuster, 1997.

Simmons, Roberta G. and Dale A. Blyth. *Moving into Adolescence: The Impact of Pubertal Change and School Context.* New York: Aldine de Gruyter, 1987.

Thorne, Barrie and Zella Luria. "Sexuality and Gender in Children's Daily Worlds," *Social Problems* 33 (1986): 176-189.

Chapter 3

Growing Accustomed to the Dark
Illness, Loss, and Grief
in the Middle School Years

Before addressing this painful subject, it is important to say that I do not presume to have the last word on suffering. However, having been through some dark places myself, particularly involving illness, loss, and grief, I come to the subject with a certain amount of experience. I first experienced the reality of loss as a child, when one of my best friends died of a rather strange illness that prevented her body from growing as it should. Thus, at my first remembered visit to a funeral home, I viewed the tiny casket of someone I had sat on the school steps with for many recesses. My second visit took place when my best friend's mother, who had suffered from depression for many years, took her own life. Both these experiences made death seem very real to me and also oddly premature. However, the most painful loss, which I experienced as an adult, was the death of my own son, Adam, at age seven. After valiantly fighting a form of kidney cancer for almost two years, he finally went to Jesus with all his fears and pain and questions forever silenced. Of course, the rest of us are left with our own struggles to make some sense out of what seemed like yet another premature parting. So, although I approach this subject with trepidation, I also come to it with credentials I would, quite frankly, rather not possess.

🌢 🌢 🌢

I once asked my eighth grade students to write about "Sufferings That Have Seasoned Me," and later I was approached at a parent/teacher conference by one girl's parents, who wanted to discuss this assignment. They were disgruntled that I required students to write on such a subject. I began my response under the assumption that they felt this subject might be too painful to write about at such a tender age. But that was not their objection. Their words come back to me with painful clarity: "How can you ask our daughter to write about a subject she knows nothing about? She hasn't *suffered* yet. She's only thirteen." My mouth did not fall open and I did not laugh, but that was the most ludicrous comment I had ever heard. I finally found the poise to reply that perhaps they were assuming I was speaking of catastrophic suffering, which is not always part of a child's experience, though sadly it all too often is. I said that *all* children suffer, whether it is from a small physical injury, or homesickness, or an emotional wound, such as being lonely or slighted or frustrated. The truth is that I have found my students do not have any trouble writing about this subject. Suffering is a reality that was ushered in with the Fall in Eden, and I believe there is a longing in the middle school years to name some of the sufferings and perhaps in the process to find a measure of understanding and healing.

Disease

> Some say it is a disease
> Some say it is a disability
> Most say it is a disadvantage
> Among only the unfortunate.
>
> I say disease is
> my life,
> my death,
> my in-between.
> I say disease is
> my hoping for tomorrow
> and longing for forever.
> I say disease is
> what I live with . . .
> deal with . . .
> fight with.

Chapter 3

The student who wrote this poem was trying to make some sense out of her life-threatening disease. Jamie was born with cystic fibrosis, and until middle school she was not especially verbal about it. Her mother kept the teachers informed. She was absent more often than most students and had a chronic cough, but she struggled to make her life as normal as possible. In middle school, poetry opened some important windows for her, and she wrote about her struggle with depth and poignancy. Many times she volunteered to read her poems aloud in class, and for some who had been with her throughout elementary school, the nature of her disease became much more real. I especially love the words *"my life, my death, my in-between"* because they state so plainly how her illness is a companion that has become part of who she is.

Here we see the need for students in middle school to confront their problems, whether they are as extreme as a life-threatening illness or as commonplace as poor social skills. Parents remain an important source of support, but as these students venture toward independence, they seem to recognize that they must grab hold of whatever problems disable them and take responsibility for addressing those problems. This recognition can result in inappropriate behavior, of course, but more often I have seen a fierce desire to identify themselves and see what repair needs to be done. In Jamie's case, the work involved being honest and forthright about her disease. As middle school teachers, we need to offer avenues for independence and communication. Writing is a strong avenue. So is drama. So is something as simple as a class discussion. But the key is for the teacher to know her students before the year gets too far along.

At our school we are privileged to have special education students included in our regular classrooms. I must admit that when this program began I had some serious reservations, not only about what I could offer such students academically but even more about what kind of odd behavior I might have to cope with in my classroom. And these fears were not unfounded, since both learning levels and behavior problems can cause struggles in inclusive education. But all children have hurdles to overcome in these two areas, so the deeper waters simply made for greater challenges, greater blessings.

One day, as I was in the midst of looking for evidence of personification in James Weldon Johnson's poem "The Creation," one of my students began waving her hand frantically. The special education student beside her was in the early stages of a seizure. I immediately rushed to her side and sent another student to find the special education teacher. I was able to get any potentially dangerous objects out of Rachel's reach, and I simply held her as she suffered through her seizure. By the time it was over, the special education teacher had come, and we asked Rachel if she wanted to go home. She preferred to rest on some pillows on the floor of our classroom until her mother arrived. Suddenly I found myself facing a decision about what to do next. Somehow returning to "business as usual" felt terribly inappropriate. So I suggested that we all pray for Rachel together, and we did. After we finished, we all turned to look at her, and she smiled wanly and waved her skinny little hand. This resulted in many open, vulnerable comments from Rachel's classmates concerning times in the past when they had been injured or sick at school. Always there was the theme of how uncomfortable and embarrassing it was to be so out-of-control in front of their peers. I would like to think the frankness of this discussion made them handle future sufferings with a little more empathy.

But these are physical sufferings, though of course they are coupled with emotional dynamics and coping mechanisms. Generally, we all handle such hardships with some measure of grace. But what happens when a student's illness is *emotional?* How interesting that we all, whether children or adults, become clumsier in handling this kind of suffering. Not long ago our middle school students were forced to face such an event, and I think it was handled gracefully.

Chapter 3

    Katlin was a beautiful, intelligent, sensitive girl. But she had suffered from many hard circumstances in her young life, and her depression in eighth grade brought everything to a climax. I have discovered that experiencing a climax during the middle school years is not unusual, although I'm not sure why. Probably it has much to do with the fact that, at this junction between childhood and adulthood, there is an unconscious need to settle some matters in order to proceed. . . . I can only speculate, since I am not a psychologist. At any rate, because of her depression, Katlin was hospitalized in a mental health clinic. For a long time students simply assumed she was sick, since Katlin was frequently absent. I went to visit her after a few days with another teacher, at her request, and I was pleased to see how well she was doing. She brought up the matter of what to tell her classmates. She wanted them to know, and yet she didn't want them to treat her like "a freak."

    After talking about our options, we came to an acceptable plan. The next day we gathered Katlin's classmates together. The other teacher, who, interestingly, had also suffered from depression and gotten help for it, began to talk to the students about what one does when he suspects he has a tumor. Obviously, he seeks professional help to diagnose the problem and probably remove the tumor. He said that the same is true of a person who is suffering from depression. Someone needs to recognize the problem and help the patient find a way to remove it. This, he said, was what happened to Katlin. After a time, when we asked for questions, it was remarkable how many hands went up. And the questions were legitimate and caring: "How should we treat her when she comes back?" "Is it OK to write her?" "Is she mad at any of us?" We emphasized how important it was to be honest about the cause of her absence and at the same time to welcome her back and keep life as normal as possible for her. Then we all prayed together. When Katlin returned, she found love and acceptance and very little awkwardness. It was a smooth transition.

Just as there are different kinds of illness, there are also different kinds of loss. Again, middle school students often find writing about loss therapeutic, and some of their best writing comes from tapping into what they remember. The following are some poems centering on this theme. Allow their beautiful voices to reveal what losses matter to them and how they feel about them:

Photograph

*Crazy what
one second and
pressing buttons
can do . . .
capturing life,
capturing beauty, love, wonder
on one glossy sheet:
colors, life,
and you.
First tooth,
baby fat,
how long my hair was,
Grandma's last birthday party . . .
Remember our old dog?
Such memories hold the
image and keep it alive:
That falling leaf never really
touched the ground.
That snowman never
really melted.*

Speaking of photographs, I have developed a ritual at the beginning of each school year that speaks volumes to me about my students, specifically and generally. Each year before school begins, I go through the available files on each student, checking for medical problems, learning disabilities, and the like. But always I end my research by looking at the folder where all this material is located. Across the top of the folder is a row of tiny school pictures for each year of the child's education. I look particularly at the eyes and mouth. And almost invariably I see bright, eager expressions in the early years that gradually become more guarded and masked as the children get older. Part of loss includes the loss of freedom to let others know who you are, because as children get more sophisticated, they also get more cruel. Part of loss is disillusionment. The fact is that the snowman *did* melt, and we wish he hadn't. . . . In middle school, we must help our students speak their regret about this reality. In the process we cannot restore that kindergarten innocence, but perhaps we can help them remove a mask or two.

Plastic Soldiers

I watch as my brother
plays war . . .
He carefully and innocently resets
the miniature plastic soldiers
in clumsy line
across the floor.
Then, in the midst of
"make-believe" when everyone
is stationed, the sound effects
of war, the bombs, the guns,
the cries begin.
Later, after his pointless little game
on the bedroom floor is finished
exciting him, he pushes the dead
aside and begins resetting
the tiny men . . .
The world is so like my
little brother, not knowing
why it creates and re-creates
life and death.
Life lost, looking for a
hopeful solution
that is never made.

What You Left Behind

Remember how you used to
be, how you used to talk
to the man-in-the-moon,
and wished on stars,
and said little prayers?

Remember when school was
just a building,
and music came out of a box?

Remember all the swing rides,
dandelions,
and sledding hills?

And remember how you
miss the little person you
left behind?

To Grandma

We would go after school—
maybe leaves to pick up
or grass to be mowed . . .

The family gatherings, with the old toys
the dark and forbidden upstairs
the flooded basement, the cluttery garage
the back steps, the front porch
the bush by the driveway . . .

Saying, "You're always welcome . . .
I got some cookies . . .
Come back soon . . ."

Like being left out in the rain
Having to leave someone so lonely.

Chapter 3

    I cannot tell you how much poetry I get about grandparents. Middle school students generally *love* their grandparents, and they are less afraid to verbalize this love than their love for their parents. At our school we have a traditional "Grandparents Day," which is a pretty big deal even for middle school students. It is touching to see how they jump up when their grandparents enter the classroom, and eagerly point to a waiting chair. Perhaps it is that unconditional, adoring acceptance they are so hungry for that makes them so eager to acknowledge these visitors. Sometimes they also recognize some striking similarities to their own plight in their grandparents' struggles with loneliness and loss in a society that does not gracefully accept them. The loss of a grandparent is a huge milestone for adolescents.

Please

Again, I have lost something
very special.
I have lost something so precious
and so real.

I have never felt so strong
or sure about anything,
and never have I been so blind.
So blind, I couldn't even see it coming—
I should have.
All the good things leave me,
even the most precious things,
they all eventually leave.

I don't know why.

Grandpa's Gone

*I remember on that bright sunny
morning in May—
the swish-swashing of the washing machine
as I sat happily watching
Saturday morning cartoons on TV.
I heard the familiar ding-a-ling
of our kitchen phone—
then my mother's soft voice
so as not to let me hear—
then click.
I ran into the kitchen
only to find my father, my hero
on the kitchen chair weeping.
Grandpa's dead,
It hit me like a brick—just that word, "dead."
Though I was too young
to understand all it meant,
I knew that my life
would never be the same.*

Dad

*I would like to ask you
how to improve my swing
or what girls' kisses
taste like
or why my mother's kisses
weren't good enough for you . . .
But the door is closed—
and you are the one
who shut it.*

A fairly recent *Grand Rapids Press* paper carried a provocative article by journalist Cal Thomas. In it he related some disturbing information based on a lengthy study of middle- and upper-class families from Marin County, California, and reported by research expert Judith Wallerstein and psychology professor Julia Lewis.

Half of the children studied became seriously involved with drugs and alcohol. Many of the children, especially girls, became sexually active early in adolescence. . . . Lewis noted that the long-lasting effects of their parents' divorce caused children to become "very very anxious about marriage [and] fidelity." ("Children of Divorce: The Cover-up Ends," 1997)

I find this study very sad and very believable. Increasingly in Christian schools, teachers are faced with students from single parent or second marriage homes. Although I have no statistics on all the effects of such home situations, I can say with certainty that I have generally found middle school students in this predicament to be less focused, less capable of meeting homework responsibilities, and less trusting of adults. At the same time, let me say that many of these students are also more sensitive than others, quicker to reach out to someone in pain, and generally more mature.

Abuse

It makes me mad when
one person's pleasure
steals another person's innocence,
when
one person's anger
steals another person's self-esteem,
when
one person's refuse
steals another person's future,
when
one person's hypocrisy
steals another person's faith.

Unfortunately, abuse is also increasingly an issue in Christian middle schools. Once again, the middle school seems to be a time when the student who has been abused is more inclined to look the experience straight in the face and find a way to come to terms with it. I have had many students who have written about abuse or have come to me and asked me to listen to their stories about abuse. Increasingly I find myself as a middle school teacher needing to be well informed about resources for reporting abuse or for finding good counseling for an abused child. And again, this pain hinders a student's ability to focus on something as seemingly mundane as schoolwork. We no longer teach in an era when academic instruction is what we are all about. We are sometimes about sorting through a whole lot of garbage before any of our lesson plans matter. We must be sensitive to this issue in order to teach effectively. Today, the scope of teaching is broader than ever before.

What do you remember losing from your childhood? Perhaps it was as simple as a child's carefree perspective on life, or perhaps it was as big as death. We have all suffered. "Nothing gold can stay."

The hardest student to say good-bye to that year was Phep. His journey was close to my heart from the beginning. I am trying to remember why. . . . Of course, there was his enthusiasm and his athletic prowess that set him apart from the others. He was literally able to be on the floor one second and on a high table beside him the next with one jump. He had springs in his feet, I told him. And he would always forget the rules, which made life hard for him sometimes. *OOPS! Can't wear a hat in class. . . . OOPS! No CD players allowed in school. . . . OOPS! That basketball is getting tossed around in the room again.* When he was reprimanded or reminded, he was always apologetic. When he had to pay the price for forgetting, he was frustrated but cooperative.

Chapter 3

    Phep fought racism on a daily basis. Mostly it was little remarks about the way he talked or read, or how shiny his hair was. He tried to laugh it off, or show off as a way of dealing with it. Sometimes he would wear his hair in a little pony tail on the top of his head in a kind of samurai warrior motif, and everyone thought it was hilariously funny. But sometimes he would come to me or another teacher and complain. Sometimes he just wanted to be taken seriously and respected like anyone else. When we offered to talk to his persecutors, he refused adamantly, saying it would just make matters worse. Nearly everyone genuinely liked Phep, but only a few took him seriously. Phep told me once that there was only one boy in the class who really knew him and listened to what he was feeling.

    About halfway through the second semester, Phep started getting more and more involved in our discussions in Bible class. He was full of questions. What made Christianity the only true religion? Was there a heaven? What was it like? Was there a hell? Why did people have to suffer? After Nate shared a story about how he had nearly died in an accident as a young child, Phep timidly shared a rare story about a Cambodian refugee camp where he nearly died of starvation and disease before coming to America. I remember we all wondered that day why God had spared each of them . . . what He had in store for them.

    I remember one kind of "communion" service we had for devotions. We lit one candle from the center "Jesus candle" and then looked into the eyes of the person beside us and offered God's peace as we lit that person's candle. I remember looking into Phep's eyes as I lit his candle. I saw Jesus there. He chose to do his final Bible project on the image of God, and he made a kind of collage of people from different races and ages and cultures reflected in a kind of mirror. He prayed aloud several times second semester, haltingly, and cautiously, but so fervently.

    At graduation, Phep and two others knelt on the steps during the performance in sign language of the Lord's Prayer. At the end he looked straight up and raised his hands high. I wondered at the time what was in his heart and mind. I have a beautiful picture someone took of him at that moment, and it is framed in my study at home. When I look at it, tears come into my eyes. I think I know what was in his heart at that moment. Yes. I think I know.

At the end of graduation, when the principal greeted the class of 1996, Phep let out a whoop of delight and frequently raised his arm "Rocky style" in celebration and victory. That night he wore a vivid deep turquoise shirt and pants. He knew he would stand out and look different, and he was starting to celebrate that difference. He told me he was going to be "really colorful" that night. He was. He was beautiful.

The next week I wrote Phep a letter and sent him a picture of the two of us at graduation. I told him that I hoped he would keep asking the important questions, and that he would hold on to the truths he had come to accept in the past year. And I told him that I loved him.

On July 20, Phep drowned in a gravel pit just outside of town. He didn't know how to swim, and when someone tried to teach him, he panicked, and he drowned. I went with another teacher and Phep's friend's parent to the house of the family. They were bewildered and screaming with the pain of their loss. Phep's father kept saying Phep was *not ever sick. . . a good ball player. . . a good boy. . . .*

> As I watch the video of graduation, I marvel again at how beautiful and active that young man in turquoise looked to all of us. How strange to think of his body now still. He was never still. He wrote on a farewell card to a departing teacher, "I will see you in heaven." So. He had made up his mind, and he knew. He just didn't know how soon his prophecy would come true. We are left behind, with all our grief and guilt and bittersweet memories of small glories. Farewell, sweet warrior. Your battle is done.

That was my journal entry shortly after Phep's death. I share it in these pages for two reasons. The first is to encourage you, if you are a middle school teacher, or intending to become

Chapter 3

one, to look at each of your students as gifts given to you for a short time. Use your time with one eye on heaven. The second is to share with you two small excerpts from letters I received later in the summer from two boys in Phep's class. Neither knew what the other had written; both letters were spontaneous. This letter speaks eloquently on how a middle school student copes with loss:

> *Every day it seems to get a little easier. Easier to live, easier to think about him, easier to think about death—almost like it's an everyday thing. Come to think of it, it IS an everyday thing. I don't know if easier is better. I don't want to forget what I've learned. . . . I will come and visit some time. I miss you, and <u>I'll see you in heaven</u>. [emphasis his]*

And this one:

> *I have decided to dedicate the cross on my neck to Phep. I will never take it off. I'm living life different now because of this. I want to try to live my life for Jesus all the time, not just sometimes. I want to put my life in His hands. I am embracing the Comforter and trying my hardest to accept His mysterious ways. . . . I can confidently say to you, "I will see you in heaven!"*

Emily Dickinson once wrote "We grow accustomed to the Dark." Illness, grief, and loss are all part of that darkness. As middle school teachers we must enter into our students' sufferings and offer ways to "fit our vision to the dark" so that their lives can "step almost straight." Anything less won't do.

For Discussion

1. What are some of the coping techniques your students have demonstrated in times of illness, loss, or grief?
2. Does your school have a policy in place regarding student reports of abuse?
3. What makes middle school especially difficult and fragile ground when it comes to issues of loss due to divorce or death?

4. What is your reaction to the parent at the beginning of this chapter who said that her daughter "hasn't suffered yet"?
5. How did you suffer in middle school? Who was there for you?

Chapter 4

Finding a Way Through Teaching in Middle School

Graduation was just two weeks away. Matt had been chosen by his eighth-grade classmates to speak at that event, which made him feel honored in February but terrified now that it was almost June. When he approached me for help, I suggested that he talk about what he had learned at our school, which is a K-8 system. I asked him to think about what he had learned socially and academically in elementary school as opposed to middle school. "Or maybe," I remember saying, "you learned the same things in both places, but in *different ways*." Allow me to share an excerpt from his speech:

> I've learned some of the same lessons over and over again throughout school, but in different ways at different stages of my growing up. In elementary school, I learned first of all about sportsmanship. We learned a lot of this through recess skills, and we needed some strong help from our elementary teachers. For example, in my case, I remember playing kickball with Justin during recess. He hit me with the ball exceptionally hard, and I was so mad that I threw it back equally hard toward his face. A teacher had to step in and talk to us about how we were being unfair to each other, about how we needed to cooperate in our playing together. . . .
>
> The second area where I learned in elementary school was discipline. I remember how much the teachers were a part of this. One teacher would become "nice bear" if we were good and "angry bear" if we were bad. Sometimes we had to write lines. I remember destroying a paper I had done poorly on in third grade in a fit of anger. I had to write over and over again: "I will not destroy my

creations." Sometimes we were disciplined by [having to put] our heads down. It didn't work very well. . . .

Still another area in elementary school was an important one, but I didn't even know I was learning about it because it came so naturally. It was in the area of pretend. On the playground a group of us would gather big branches and build a shelter so that it could be our house. We would try to sweep it out with other smaller branches. We didn't know it, but we were learning to imitate adults.

And the last area has to do with relationships. In elementary school we played with EVERYONE. If you had a birthday party, all the boys (or girls) were invited. Our parents encouraged this and were very much a part of our relationships. And we wanted to spend time with our parents too, because we needed them to set the rules for us. I remember being afraid to leave my parents to go overnight to a friend's house. At school, when our parents weren't around, we wanted our teachers to step in. Elementary teachers listen to a lot of "tattletale" stories. We depended on them for justice. . . .

But now take a look at <u>the same lessons relearned in middle school</u> [emphasis added]. Sportsmanship was more organized and sophisticated. Now a referee was given the job of deciding what was fair, and we were taught not to question his judgment. Maybe because he was an outsider, we let his word stand, and we were more afraid of him. And our playing became more structured learning. We had to develop skills in playing rather than just playing for the fun of it.

In the area of discipline, everything took on a new perception. Now we were learning SELF-discipline. Instead of watching television at night, you studied for a test—or else. I learned this from some sad experience. We had to learn to gauge our time—no more carefree endless hours of play. Pretending took on new meaning in middle school. The play helped me in that respect. I had to work at being someone else. I had to discover more about someone I was trying to be, and sometimes I found out that part of me was very much like that person.

Chapter 4

> *And finally, in relationships, tattletale behavior became unacceptable. The rule in middle school is, "Don't snitch if you want friends." Somehow we became more selective somewhere between fifth and sixth grade. We became better friends with a smaller group of people. It was good because we got to really know some people better than ever, but I also think it's kind of sad because you lost some of your friends from elementary school. . . . Parents are still important, but you choose to be with your friends over them. Your parents become a more distant "cheering section." Teachers are people you might trust, if they encourage you to think about important things—you know, bigger things, because the world is bigger. I can recall huge discussions on the "big bang" theory in science or the reality of angels in Bible [class]. . . .*

Matt's words are helpful to me as a middle school teacher. I think he is perceptive about the difference between elementary school and middle school. A good middle school teacher must recognize that middle school marks a huge change in a student's life. Students are stepping outside the carefully structured, carefully supervised world of childhood into the pre-adult world. Because it is "in between" childhood and adulthood, middle school contains a lot of murkiness. Everything is being redefined. Friends are becoming selective, which can cause never-to-be-forgotten pain; sports are becoming competitive, meaning more selectivity; parents are looking less like advocates; and teachers . . . well, teachers are tested for what possible good they might be in the midst of all this change.

Robert Frost once wrote, "The best way is always through." So a middle school teacher must jump into the murky water with his students in order to offer a life preserver. The life preserver has several things written on it. I like to think that the themes of my literature units are key themes for middle school as well. These themes could be stamped on the life preserver: Fighting Dragons, Winning, New Perceptions, Without Knowing Why, and Survival. And through all the stories and poetry and novels and writing assignments I give my students, there must be this thread of connection to the world they are now living in. Otherwise they will dismiss me. And I will deserve dismissal.

So what *works* in teaching middle school? I have a small sign in my room, which I put on a wall beneath a remarkable pencil drawing from one of my former students. The drawing is of a fishbowl with a rather wary-looking fish swimming in it. Two beautiful, strong, detailed hands hold the fishbowl. The sign I place beneath this drawing says, "It all begins with relationship." And that is the strongest truth I can offer here. If a relationship between teacher and student is established, then almost anything can happen. Without a strong relationship, there will be little learning of any kind.

Ingredients of a Strong Relationship

When I tell someone I teach middle school, invariably the question is asked, "How do you manage to keep them in line? It's such a *difficult* age." And, as Matt wrote in his graduation speech, discipline is an important lesson in life. A teacher needs to draw for her students a line they may not cross. Every teacher knows this. However, I think that in drawing the line, a middle school teacher needs to make some allowances for the physical and emotional clumsiness of her students. As I said, this is murky water. The starkness of black and white disappears in the land of middle school. So I say to students, if you speak out of turn, I will warn you, and if you speak out of turn again, the ax will fall. If you make fun of someone, I will take you aside and try to make you walk in that person's moccasins. But if you persist, I will make you spend noon hour with me in silence. If you bounce a basketball in my room during lunch hour and knock over someone's milk, you will clean up the milk and be told to bounce your basketball on a basketball court. But if it bounces into my room again, with or without spilled milk, the ball will become mine for a few weeks. The first offense is a mistake, and needs to be treated as such; chances are the second offense is a test, and you as a teacher must not miss the opportunity to pass with flying colors. The obvious benefit of

Chapter 4

drawing such a line is that generally there is peace in the classroom. More importantly, I have encouraged trust because I mean what I say, and you know what to expect. *But when the ax falls it never never never humiliates.*

A second ingredient of a strong relationship is praise. Of course, we all love to be praised, but in middle school particularly, when the self-image is usually rather shaky, praise is especially welcome. But praise must be legitimate and specific, and this requires looking at the individual students and seeing where their gifts lie. This involves NAMING each student, not to categorize but to fertilize. Lindsay is an actress, and I must find ways for her to express that gift, not only in the school play but also within class activities. . . . read this part aloud, Lindsay. Caleb is a clown, and his humor can be directed toward establishing a relaxed atmosphere for sharing ideas without feeling threatened. Tim loves order, so he can be given responsibility for assigning roles to students in group work. If you have wisely and carefully named your students, they will allow you to lead them into taking risks they might have previously avoided. I remember Brian. By some fluke, he was put into an Exploratory that he had not signed up for, one he dreaded most, a Drama Exploratory! Brian was shy and quiet; often he would have preferred to be invisible. He resigned himself to staying in the class because a friend was there.

Actually, Brian had incredible timing and great facial expression, and as he relaxed with the other students, all making delightful fools of themselves, he proved himself a good performer. The long and short of it was that Brian tried out for and made the school play—not a huge part but a pivotal one. His mother was *shocked*. But Brian had decided that "actor" was a name he could live with, and even enjoy.

And finally, a third ingredient of a strong relationship is humor. Humor is a great gift. If you can laugh at yourself, it will ease much of your pain and stress. I have found that the teachers who have the most difficulty in middle school have trouble laughing at themselves. Middle school is a place where you

Knol

cannot *survive* without laughter. When I think of the times I've made a fool of myself in front of my students, I am grateful that I don't generally take myself too seriously. In middle school, the smallest errors are either shattering or hilarious. At the risk of sounding crass, I will use the example of "passing gas." For some odd reason, this is one of the most outrageously funny events in the life of a middle school student. Someone who gets into this embarrassing situation immediately does one of two things: turns crimson and pretends someone else nearby did it, or falls on the floor in convulsive laughter as everyone else runs for the windows. The former will result in teasing off and on for the remainder of the day; the latter will be forgotten as soon as the teacher reestablishes order.

At the same time, you as a teacher must be able to laugh at yourself. Valentine's Day is a big deal in middle school. All week we have "secret cupids," who give little gifts and notes to each other, and at the end of the week we have a party. A few years ago, I had some heart-shaped balloons that I hung from the lights in my room for Valentine's Day. They had to hang upside-down because, of course, the tie-off of each balloon was at the bottom of the heart, where you attach the string. Now use your imagination to picture what upside-down hearts hanging from the fluorescent lights look like from below. . . . My first hour class was restless, and I couldn't imagine why. Then, as I followed the last student into my room at the beginning of second hour, I heard him say (not knowing I was behind him), "Hey, look at that! Hanging boobs!" You laugh or you cry. (Fortunately, I laughed until tears ran down my cheeks. Unfortunately, I told the story in the teacher's lounge at break, and as I began teaching the next hour, I saw several teachers poking their heads into my classroom. . . . Middle school teachers are more warped than most!)

What are some learning techniques that work well in middle school? The answers are as varied as the individual teachers, of course. But having laid the foundation for the all-important realm of relationship, let's look at some techniques that contribute to the

Chapter 4

formation of relationships and to greater knowledge of ourselves and the world around us.

On the first day of school, I hand out a rather intimidating writing assignment called "The Conclusion." I take no credit for the idea of this assignment beyond redesigning it to fit a middle school English class setting. It was created by Anthony de Mello, author of *Wellsprings: A Book of Spiritual Exercises* (New York: Doubleday, 1984) and was originally intended as a kind of exercise for personal devotions. I use it as a kind of autobiographical creative writing assignment. Each "chapter" is two to three pages long, and I give the students the chapter titles. For example, one chapter students write about is "These experiences I have cherished." Another is "These risks I have taken." Another large chapter involves the senses, "These things I have smelled . . . heard . . . seen . . . touched." Allow me to share some student examples:

THESE THINGS I HAVE SMELLED . . .

The most wonderful smell in the world is that of my grandmother. Everything she owns smells of it, and that smell will never go away. I know it's the smell of her perfume, but I like to think of it as her smell. It's as if it was made with her in mind, and only intended for her to wear. The perfume just doesn't fit on anyone else. It sticks out like a sore thumb. It won't accept anyone else. The smell is not of flowers, or any earthly thing. The fresh, clean smell of the world after it has been washed clean by the rain is the only thing that comes close. That doesn't even do it justice, though. It's the smell of my grandmother, and I'll leave it at that. Anyone else wearing it reeks of a bold imposter. . . .

THESE THINGS I HAVE HEARD . . .

One part of life that is most important to me is hearing. I find it amazing what you can learn by just sitting and listening to people. Everyone should try it. Hearing things is really the key to understanding things.

One sound I enjoy, yet it can really grate on me, is the ticking of a clock. The rhythmic, precise ticking makes me feel secure. It keeps on ticking, without fail, every second, minute, hour, day. . . . I like the faithfulness of this sound as long as I'm not trying to concentrate or trying to sleep. . . .

A sound that sends shivers up my spine is that of a siren. Sirens are and always will be linked to bad things. When I hear a siren, thoughts flash through my mind. Is that siren heading to pick up someone I know, or a complete stranger? Who is now going to be without a mother or father or child? Is there anyone to cry for the person? Maybe no one is hurt at all; maybe it's a high-speed chase. Down the highway two cars race, one trying to get away, the other pursuing the lawbreaker. Maybe that happens more on television than in real life. There could be a fire blazing while we go about our day unaware. People's lives may be getting ruined while we talk and laugh with our friends. When I hear a siren, all these thoughts go through my mind. Then I get distracted and go about my daily routine. I never again stop and think about what was connected to the siren. Until now.

THIS BOOK HAS LEFT AN IMPRESSION ON ME . . .

One book that has strongly impressed me is <u>The Miracle Worker</u>. I was blown away at how intelligent Helen Keller was, even though she was blind and deaf at the age of eighteen months. It showed me that no matter what your circumstances are, you should never give up and just go for whatever glory there is out there. It also showed me love and how love needs to be strong and disciplined. Sometimes this book made me feel like I understood what it would be like to be both blind and deaf. If I was blind or deaf I would be overjoyed to see and hear for a few days, or even for a few seconds. I would appreciate God's creation so much more. People who don't suffer from these handicaps get bored with trees, flowers, animals, and all the sounds they make, but people who are blind and deaf would never find these boring. They would be thankful for every detail they could see.

Chapter 4

THESE ARE SOME SIGNIFICANT ADULTS IN MY LIFE . . .

I have a negative influence to write about. I think one of the reasons why I have always been so shy around adults, teachers in particular, is because I really didn't know or trust them. Now that I am older and wiser, I would like to go back to one of the teachers I had as a little child and tell her that I privately called her "the witch." I would like to tell her that she made me feel dumb, stupid, and worthless. I thought I had to cheat in order to arrive at answers because when I asked her for help she would just hit me on the head with her knuckle, and she would say "Think, think, think—that's what your brain is for!" Now I think that I have something to say and that I am even smart in some areas, and I have gained confidence. I wish I had the confidence to tell her that she labeled me "stupid" but I'm not stupid, and I hope she doesn't ever do that to a student again.

THESE ARE SOME REGRETS I HAVE . . .

We all have regrets, big and small, too many to count, but some come to mind more than others. I regret not listening to my grandpa's stories with more intent as I got older. My grandpa died recently; he was old and had had a stroke earlier in life. When he was young, he was kind of a "tough guy." He was the type who was always told by adults that he wouldn't live to see thirty. He started smoking at age twelve, and he rode a motorcycle. My grandma, on the other hand, was the quiet type. She was a good "school girl," and she was sort of frightened yet intrigued by my grandpa.

Somehow they found each other and got married. My grandpa quit smoking, but he still had a stroke when he got older. I think his regret chapter would certainly start with smoking. When he was an old man, he told me stories of when he was little, and as a younger child I listened intently because he was a great storyteller. But as I got older, I listened less because I had heard the stories before. After he died, I wished I had listened better because I would never get to hear them from his lips again.

I find this assignment one of the most valuable I give, for several reasons. First, it is "a way in" for students, parents, and teachers together. Students take time to ponder what has been important so far in their lives, and then they articulate that into something beautiful, often profound. Parents are overwhelmed by what is inside their children, and the paper often becomes an occasion for remembering and communicating. As a teacher, I have the precious opportunity of getting acquainted with my students early in the year, learning about not only their writing skills but more importantly who they are and what they see. Second, it is a powerful time management tool. I give my students a calendar that suggests ways to divide the assignment into "small bites" so they aren't overwhelmed. It is one of their first tastes of using their time well *on their own*, since I never give class time for this assignment. Remember Matt's comment about middle school as a place where you learn more *self-discipline*? And finally, in this age of keeping portfolios for each grade, each paper is a telling manuscript that captures the mind and heart of an eighth grader.

Before I go on, let me insert a point that is extremely important to me. As I share this idea with other English teachers, I am always surprised to find one or more who consider this assignment far too ambitious for a middle school student. My response is that it is probably too much for a seventh grader. However, I think that eighth grade is the perfect year for it, as students are on the brink of high school. At the same time, I cannot emphasize enough my belief that one of the greatest disservices we do to our students is to have low expectations for them. Obviously, students of widely varying abilities will be writing the paper, but the assignment is *available to them at whatever level they are able to embrace it.* I have had gifted students who wrote chapters of ten pages or more, and I have had struggling students, even special education students, write a single page or paragraph. But it is a challenge that nearly always excites them, and it is with an air of near reverence that they place their final document on my desk. We teachers must never

Chapter 4

water things down. We give the kite and string to all our students, and then we see how high each one can fly.

Journaling is another teaching tool that can be useful, and it need not be limited to English class. A friend of mine who teaches math uses a journal as an avenue for students to talk about how they solve math problems and what makes math easier for them. A science teacher can use journals to help students step from the lab experiment to the application or significance of their conclusions. One important matter teachers should discuss with each other is the need to be careful not to use the journal in the same way all the time. In my seventh-grade English class I use journals primarily as a response to the novels we read. However, in my eighth-grade class, I use them more often to lead into the themes of stories and poems we study. When I teach creative writing, I use journals for small writing exercises. Again, let me share a small journal piece from an eighth grader. I gave the assignment just before we studied an Emily Dickinson poem about parting. I gave my students a single word to play with for ten minutes. The word was *good-bye*:

> *"Good-bye" can be a sad word because there are so many things we don't want to part with. But it is not too sad, because it means that you are giving someone your blessing upon parting. So it is probably used more for positive moments because we stop to say "goodbye" when there was a relationship that mattered. It is also not as final as "farewell" or "I'll miss you" because it need not indicate a long period of absence. What I notice is that "goodbye" means someone is leaving, for however long, and so does "bye." But a simple "bye" has no blessing, just a dismissal. It is quick and painless, and it seems to be saying "take a hike." But "goodbye" means "have a good trip."*

And then there is the matter of classroom atmosphere. Obviously, this results mainly from what goes on in the classroom, but I for one think the room itself is important. We are such visual people, and some of us are primarily visual learners. Recently our family spent a week in England, and while there, we worshiped at St. Margaret's Cathedral in Westminster Abbey. After being surrounded by the images of that remarkable place, I wrote the following in my journal:

> An odd parallel, perhaps, but the way the church was so "busily" beautiful and all made me think of my classroom back home. I choose what goes into that place so carefully, just as the "cathedral people" do here, wanting each thing to have significance and its proper location. . . .

And so, as I prepare my classroom at the beginning of each year, it is very much like a gift that I offer to my students. It is full of visuals, not chosen haphazardly—never haphazardly, because the result would be overstimulating and less purposeful. So this is my "Drama Corner," and here you will find collages of past plays, and posters about performance, and a porcelain tragedy/comedy drama mask. And the back wall is my Bible "Art Gallery," filled with pictures students drew in a collaborative art/Bible project, each one carefully framed and hung. And on those huge blank white walls above my windows, my dear husband has hand-painted quotations I selected—one from Mother Teresa about doing small things with great love, and one from C. S. Lewis about Aslan not being safe but being good, and a favorite verse from Psalm 31 about our times being in God's hands. On my desk is a lamp given me by a wise and generous friend. It is called a "redemption lamp," and is made entirely of "junk"—glass and iron from the dump—junk turned into something beautiful, just as we are beautiful because of Jesus' sacrifice. And the first thing that always comes out each year is a small framed quotation from Emily Dickinson: "Take care, for God is here." That is where I must always begin.

So my classroom is beautiful, because our surroundings either depress or inspire us, don't they? Let me close this rather lengthy chapter by listing and commenting briefly on a few other teaching techniques that can be considered because they have "worked":

Chapter 4

Leave the premises on occasion.

It's funny how much students remember those times when they left their classrooms in order to learn. One teacher I know was about to explore Jesus' powerful "Sermon on the Mount" in Matthew. It was a beautiful day, so he took his class to a grassy hillside near school and "preached" the beatitudes. The class discussed not only what Jesus said but what His audience might have been thinking as they listened to Him.

Some great poetry is written in cemeteries. Or on playground equipment.

Try a spatial writing exercise in the hallway, with each student looking at the inside of her locker.

Assign students a familiar place to examine, looking for details they never noticed before. It's remarkable how much better their senses work at such times.

For Christian service, go to a rest home, a shelter that feeds the homeless, or another agency that offers assistance in the local community.

Go to a play, especially if your students are about to perform their own.

Integrate subject areas wherever you can but only if it can be done naturally and effectively.

Forced integration is worthless. In my Bible class we attempt to define certain biblical concepts like mercy, or miracle, or sacrifice [see chapter 6]. In art class students were about to begin a unit on drawing hands. So we two teachers put our heads together and decided to have as their final art project a drawing of hands to illustrate one of the Bible words. As an English teacher, I am pleased to say that they each wrote a paragraph explaining what inspired their drawing. The results were remarkable!

Use storytelling whenever you can, in whatever subject you teach.

We never outgrow our love for stories. In history, for example, people's lives reveal a great deal about their historical setting. Take students behind the scenes with some of those English kings, showing what brought them to the place where they shaped history. A novel like Cynthia Rylant's *I Had Seen Castles* is a powerful way to teach World War II, revealing the desperation and fear the common people felt over the state of the world. Again, storytelling can be used effectively in any subject area.

On the same note, even though middle school students have left childhood behind, they still love games as long as they are not condescending.

The "Jeopardy" concept is a way to review for a test. Your classroom can become a courtroom as you teach about the judicial system. Grammar review can become a bingo game. Your students can act out in mime a story like O. Henry's "The Cop and the Anthem." You can teach the basics of debate through a short story or novel that presents opposing points of view, such as Ray Bradbury's "The Flying Machine" or Richard Wright's "Hunger." They are learning as they play.

The best way is *through*. It begins with relationship. Come prepared. Let them teach you.

Laugh well. Don't condescend. Aim high. *Anything can happen.*

For Discussion

1. Is teaching harder today than it was ten years ago? Explain.
2. What have you done that works well in engaging your students' attention and interest?
3. How, and how much, do you take into account your students' different learning styles?
4. How has your sense of humor helped you as a teacher?

Chapter 5
What Are We Supposed to Teach? Designing a Middle School Curriculum

In *What Your Sixth Grader Needs to Know,* E. D. Hirsch tells of a mother who wrote to him expressing her dismay that her identical twin children, in different rooms of the same grade in the same school, were learning completely different things. Hirsch says that this situation happens when schools lack a definite, specific curriculum. When Hirsch speaks of curriculum, he clearly means the shared core of knowledge and skills that students should acquire at a given grade level.

Hirsch's series, one book each for kindergarten through grade six, contains what he and a group of teachers believe is the best curriculum content for each grade level if students are to become culturally literate. The books are interesting, and it is well worth any teacher's time to examine the curriculum content his group suggests.

However, if teachers look only at Hirsch's ideas about how curriculum should be developed, they will fall into the trap that brain researchers Renate and Geoffrey Caine describe (1997). They warn that to treat information like a commodity is to believe in the following three principles:
1. Only experts create knowledge.
2. Teachers deliver knowledge in the form of information.
3. Children are graded on how much of the information they have stored. (p. 60)

The Caines say that this is not the way real learning happens. Instead, each student must make his or her own understanding of the truths that exist, and children do that at different times and in different ways. Still, erroneous as these principles are, the effects of these beliefs are everywhere in schools. Educators such as John Goodlad, Ted Sizer, Michael Fullan, and Heidi Hayes Jacobs direct us toward finding new ways of arranging curriculum so that what and how students are taught is in keeping with the way they actually learn.

How is curriculum content planned for a Christian middle school? How does a teaching staff decide which facts and skills are essential for all students to have by the time they leave a given grade level? Is it appropriate that the facts and skills taught in grade seven in one Christian school are different from those taught at that level in another school?

Whatever our answers to these questions, in many schools curriculum is whatever the teachers in each school decide it should be. And so they select a textbook in each discipline for each grade and have the students work their way through that book. What happens in many schools, including many Christian middle schools, is that the authors and publishers of the textbooks determine what the students will study and learn about a subject at each grade level.

Why isn't that sufficient? Surely the textbooks are written by experts in each field, and those experts must know what is appropriate for children and young people to know at each grade level. The truth of the matter is that textbooks are written to sell, particularly to be selected from a limited number of choices by the textbook committees of states with large populations. Often the result is that the textbook presents a great deal of information in rather sketchy ways, and teachers using it find themselves teaching for breadth instead of depth.

Each state and province has standards or benchmarks that schools are to use to assure that students are learning the content they ought to be learning. However, the benchmarks are often stated so broadly that curriculum and assessment can move in various directions. Even when two Christian middle schools in the same state use the same benchmarks as a guide in planning their curriculum, the resulting curriculum for the two schools may well be quite different.

Chapter 5

The Purpose of the Curriculum

Ernest Boyer says curriculum ought to flow from the answers we give to the question, "What kind of person, citizen, and society do we want to produce in our school?" That question is important and must be addressed in Christian schools, but the purpose of the Christian school curriculum is even larger. It is twofold: (1) to help students understand God's world, and (2) to help students understand themselves and their place in God's world. All that is to be done in ways that are appropriate to students' developmental level.

People are created to be curious. We are made that way so that we will come to understand much of that marvelous creation we call God's world. Even the parts of it we will never interact with, we want to understand. God wants us to know and understand much of the creation because all of creation speaks of God. The more we know about creation, the more we will stand in awe and wonder, so that when we see pictures of fantastically colorful fish that live deep in ocean, we will say, "I wonder what God intended when He made those fish that way? Not many people will see them. Was God just having fun?" or "I wonder why God made the baby kangaroo so tiny and vulnerable. He could have made it to be more fully developed when it is first born. It looks something like a big worm. I wonder about that."

Sometimes, through serious study and careful watching, people come to understand what God intended; other times it remains a mystery. In her book *Approaches to a Philosophical Biology,* Marjorie Grene (1968) gives the following examples of such mysteries. We know that the enormity of the male peacock's colorful fan functions in courtship, attracting the female. But on the feathers of that fan is a whole intricacy of patterns that seem not to have much function at all. Again, think of the black pattern on the wing of the mother-of-pearl butterfly. Although the size and background color are necessary for mating behavior, the detailed black pattern on the wing is beautiful and different for each butterfly, but it has no function

Reaching and Teaching Young Adolescents

we know of. Think of sea snails. Each one's shell is unique, different from the others. The variations and arrangements of colors can have no significance for the snails, which have no eyes. Their colors don't serve to attract other snails, yet they exist. In these cases and many others, we can only wonder why God added all those patterns that seem to have no function but are so interesting and beautiful to us.

God made us curious in part so that we will come to know this world we live in. God made us curious also so that we will wonder about our Creator and in our wondering will praise Him more and more, even when we don't find the answers to our wondering.

But the other purpose of curriculum is equally important—that students will come to know their own place in this world. We want each middle school student to be able to say, "I know my place is small, but I know myself as a child of God. I know the kinds of intelligence I have, and I know my gifts. I know how I am to relate to others as a child of God, and what I am to do and be in this world God has made for me to live in."

When we think back to Boyer's question concerning what kind of person, citizen, and society we want to produce in our schools, we might answer as follows:

1. Students who leave our schools will have learned to unwrap the gifts God has given them. These gifts may be intellectual, spiritual, ethical, interpersonal, intrapersonal, aesthetic, spatial, or physical. Unwrapping these gifts means developing their aptitudes and interests, and discovering the wonderful diversity that makes each of us unique.
2. Students who leave our schools will be people who have learned that living in a Christ-centered community means sharing each other's joys and burdens. This is more than pious talk. This kind of living is doing.
3. Students who leave our schools will have learned to ask questions and seek answers in a framework that incorpo-

Chapter 5

rates every area of life. The guiding questions of this framework are:
- What might have been God's intentions for this part of creation when He created it?
- Is this part of creation the way God intended it to be? If it is broken, what went wrong?
- What ought we Christians to be doing to try to bring this part of creation back to God's intention for it?

4. Students who leave our schools will have learned to think about their learning. They will be able to evaluate their learning and determine how they can build on it.
5. Students who leave our schools will have learned to be committed to seeking God's shalom—His peace, mercy, and justice—in school and in society.
6. Students who leave our schools will have developed a Christian view of life and reality.
7. Students who leave our schools will have an idea of how they can best use their gifts.

The clear and compelling purposes of the school should be kept before the teachers and students at all times, written in large letters on a poster in the room where the teachers do most of their lesson planning and on bulletin boards in the hallway. As teachers plan their instructional units, they must keep asking themselves and one another how the various activities help to reach a particular goal within the larger purpose.

Planning the Curriculum

The larger purposes of the school are carried out in the curriculum. But how can we know what particular facts, skills, and attitudes should make up the instruction at each grade level? Topics for the curriculum must be large enough to meet the requirements of outside agencies as well as the needs of students. The curriculum must be planned so that it will (1) satisfy the state or provincial standards for that level,

(2) address the personal concerns of students, (3) address the common issues people face or will face in society (often the same as the students' personal concerns), and (4) increase the students' understanding of God's creation.

Recognizing the need to meet these four goals, all the middle school teachers should work together to determine the topics to be studied at each grade level. They may decide to examine different books in the Core Knowledge Series (Hirsch, 1993) in order to determine which content recommended by Hirsch's group should be part of their own curriculum.

The teachers will then identify what skills to teach at each grade level, what skills have already been taught, and what skills should be maintained. The skills will include, among others, interviewing, summarizing, writing essays, conducting research, citing sources accurately, knowing different ways of studying, and knowing how to select the appropriate format for particular projects, including writing, presenting and supporting oral arguments, inferring, reading critically, and participating in small-group interactions.

Next, the teachers should identify the "habits of the heart," or heart attitudes, that reflect the broad purposes of the Christian middle school and should be emphasized there. Perhaps we want them to leave our school with these attitudes:

- Christians must work hard for justice and must struggle, if necessary, to see that justice prevails.
- It is extremely important to develop one's own gifts as much as possible.
- Christian students must take responsibility for others around them so that all students will be academically successful and socially accepted, and no student will feel excluded.
- It is important to take care of one's body in order to keep it as well as possible, eating nutritious foods and avoiding smoking and the use of drugs or alcohol.

How can we come to know student concerns so that answering them becomes part of curriculum content? In *A Vision With*

Chapter 5

A Task, Stronks and Blomberg suggest the following:
    One way to determine students' concerns is to ask them to write answers to these questions:

[handwritten margin note: Care Groups]

    What do you think is God's purpose for human beings?
    What keeps you from fulfilling that purpose perfectly?
    What questions do you have about yourself?
    What do you think is wrong with the world?
    What questions and concerns do you have about the world?

After the students have written their answers, have them move into small groups to see whether sharing their responses leads them to additional questions. Then present all the questions on an overhead transparency and have the class identify common questions and concerns. Those concerns should become matters for study in units where they seem to fit the best. Teachers should realize, however, that if they ask students what they would like to know, those issues that a number of students identify must become part of the unit studies if possible.

In a recent survey of middle school students in Christian schools, the student questions listed below either became unit topics or were included as part of integrated unit studies. Almost all these questions could be researched and answered by students in the study of a thematic unit on justice, wellness, relationships, identity, intelligence, or community:

- How do we know that our own religion is the true religion? (identity or community)
- How do we know that our denomination is the best one to belong to? (identity or community)
- How should it affect our lives if we were to live in global interdependence? (justice or relationships)
- What is cultural diversity, and how does it affect our lives? (justice)
- How can we know whether a war is being fought for right or wrong purposes? (justice)
- How do people come to know things? (intelligence)

- What will the world be like when we are adults? (community)
- Can people ever really create a just society? (justice)
- What kinds of careers and jobs will people have when we are adults? (identity or community)
- How much money does a family need in order to live? (justice)
- What do we need to know about sex and health? (wellness)
- What is the role of genetics in medicine and in our lives? (wellness)
- What does it mean to be intelligent? (intelligence)
- What kinds of discrimination have there been throughout history? (justice)
- What were the 1960s like? (community)
- What were the 1930s like? (community)
- What causes people to hurt other people physically or emotionally? (community)

At this point the teachers have three kinds of lists in front of them: content, skills, and attitudes. Next, they might select several large topics and decide on the grade levels in which units on those topics will be taught. Perhaps they will decide to repeat a topic; for example, they will teach a unit on justice in grade six and again in grade eight with different content. The point is that all the teachers will decide together what content will be part of each unit on justice so that overlapping or redundancy will occur only when appropriate and not by accident. The same is true for the skills. Perhaps the lists of attitudes will remain the same for each grade level.

The teachers will continue sketching these units with broad strokes until they have found a place in the middle school grades for what they believe should be taught and learned there. Once they have identified content, skills, and attitudes for each grade level, and once they have written the objectives, the teachers of that grade will have to decide what kinds of units are appropriate to meet those objectives.

Chapter 5

The Place of Disciplinary, Interdisciplinary, and Integral Units

Next, teachers are ready to discuss the balance between disciplinary, interdisciplinary, and integral units. No single kind of unit is appropriate for instruction in all areas, so teachers must decide which knowledge, skills, and attitudes are learned best through each kind of unit. Using different kinds throughout each week requires creative and flexible scheduling, but it is important to note that such scheduling is becoming increasingly common in middle schools. The kinds of units used most often in middle school classrooms are disciplinary and interdisciplinary.

Disciplinary Units

This is the kind of unit found most often in traditional classrooms. It is oriented toward one specific subject, normally making use of a textbook. When such a unit is richly taught, the teacher attempts to show students how the content of one course relates to that of other courses (Jacobs, 1989). For example, when Milt Van Drunen of Lansing Christian School in Illinois teaches the Civil War or the Revolutionary War, the students study the textbook materials, but they also develop interesting projects and present them to parents and grandparents in an evening program. They learn the war songs of the era, make hardtack, make a simple musket, and learn the basics of marching and drilling. Each student prepares a poster display or an oral presentation on weapons, medical treatment, food, important battles, or women in the war. When a disciplinary unit is taught less richly, little attempt is made to show relationships.

Advantages: The disciplinary unit is most common, and students, teachers, and parents are used to it. State and provincial goals and objectives are available for many subject areas through all grades. Middle school teachers with training in secondary schools generally have a college major in one content area and are comfortable with teaching it.

Disadvantages: Teaching by means of disciplinary units often has a fragmenting effect on students' learning. It does not reflect the wonderfully connected nature of reality, and students may fail to make connections the teacher assumes are being made, so their learning is incomplete.

Interdisciplinary Units

The interdisciplinary unit involves a view of knowledge and an approach to curriculum that consciously applies methodology and language from various disciplines to examine a central theme, issue, problem, topic, or experience (Jacobs, 1989). At times one week is set aside when all five days are used for the unit. At other times a longer block is set aside, and the unit requires several weeks of study.

Advantages: The interdisciplinary unit is stimulating and motivating for teachers and students. It helps students understand relationships between subject areas. When it is planned carefully and taught well, knowledge and skills become part of the student and are retained.

Disadvantages: This way of teaching requires effort and change. When such a unit is poorly planned, topics are included simply for the sake of "covering" a particular discipline. Also, such a unit requires time for team planning and changes in the regular school schedule. When they teach the unit in one intensive week, teachers are often so exhausted at the end that they are not easily persuaded to plan other interdisciplinary units. Parents may view that week as something other than "real learning," since interdisciplinary units were not part of their own school experience.

Integral Units

The teachers carefully examine a central theme, issue, problem, topic, or experience in order to determine what learning and activities are central to it. They help students see the connections that must be made if they are to understand that topic (Stronks and Blomberg, 1993). Teachers begin by planning the learning objectives for the unit. Next, they plan learning activities through which those objectives will be reached. No subject or discipline is included simply in order to "cover" an area. Only the learning and activities that are integral

Chapter 5

to the topic will be part of the unit. A block of time is set aside over a period of several weeks for the unit study.

Advantages: The advantages are the same as those of the interdisciplinary approach. In addition, each learning activity is carefully examined as to whether it is a valuable way of carrying out the objectives. Therefore, there is more authenticity to the instruction, and instructional time is used more effectively. Real learning is much more likely to occur, and for this reason we prefer the integral unit over the interdisciplinary unit. Parents who question whether real learning is taking place can easily be shown the scope and sequence chart of facts and skills.

Disadvantages: The teachers will have to plan their entire curriculum, including content, skills, and attitudes, creating a scope and sequence chart that shows where each will be taught or maintained in grades six, seven, and eight. This work is difficult and time consuming since it means arranging team planning time and changing the daily school schedule.

We repeat that no single kind of unit can meet all the instructional needs of middle school students. Very likely the curriculum content can best be taught with a combination of disciplinary, interdisciplinary, and integral units. For example, even in schools where the teachers are strongly committed to teach as much of the curriculum content as possible with integral units because they believe that is the best way for students to understand the connections, the decision is often made to teach mathematics through disciplinary units. Applied math still has an important place in the integral unit, but because of its sequential nature, mathematics is also taught through disciplinary units as a separate subject. The same is true of foreign language instruction.

Planning Integral Units

When teachers are planning an integral unit, it is important that they not omit any step. Parents, other teachers, and the principal have the right to know what the intentions for the unit are and what the students will actually learn. If possible, the specifics of each unit should be stored on a computer disk. As the unit is taught, appropriate changes, which always grow out of good teaching, can be added to the disk. When this happens, new teachers will be helped to understand how teachers in your school plan their instruction. Here are the steps in planning an integral unit:

   1. Unit topic The topic should arise from personal concerns of students, from common issues people face in society, from the state guidelines, and from knowledge that teachers believe will increase students' understanding of God's creation. Consider the following questions: If this aspect of the world were perfect and the way God intended it to be, what would it be like? How have the effects of sin distorted this purpose? How may we work to heal and remedy what has gone wrong?

   2. Relationships Show how this unit relates to the students' earlier learning and their later educational experiences. In other words, explain how and why the unit fits into the school curriculum.

   3. Course objectives Begin planning the unit with the end in mind. What exactly do you intend the students to learn through this unit? Be sure the objectives clearly reflect the basic theme and answer these questions: At the end of this unit, what content will the students know? What skills will they have gained or maintained? What values and attitudes do we hope the students will have?

   4. Activities Brainstorm together to identify a large assortment of interesting, worthwhile activities that will help the students fulfill the learning objectives for the unit. Then examine the activities and eliminate any that were included simply to represent a particular discipline or subject area. Mark each activity with the number of the objective or objectives it will help to fulfill. Eliminate activities that are "neat ideas" but do not help to fulfill a learning objective.

   In each unit at least one activity should be planned that will engage the students' emotions. Often it is through such activities that the intended values and attitudes are formed. In addition, if the students are to come to know about some occupations

Chapter 5

related to this area of study, at least one activity should be planned for that purpose.

5. Examination of the activities Determine whether engagement in the activities planned will ensure that all the learning objectives will be fulfilled. If not, add the necessary activities. Finally, arrange the activities as follows:

    a. *Introductory activity* This first activity is used to determine what knowledge the students already have about the topic, to arouse their interest in the unit, and to set the tone.

    b. *Developmental activities* List all activities that might be used to develop content (information), skills (thinking, research, social), and attitudes.

    c. *Culminating activity* Plan a final group activity that provides a synthesis of the information, skills, and values the unit is intended to teach.

For each activity identify content, skill, and attitude objectives. Plan activities that will be appropriate for the students' varied interests, abilities, and learning styles.

6. Assessment Determine how you will know whether the expected learning has taken place. Ways of assessing student learning may include portfolios, demonstrations, exhibits, or tests. Chapter 7 will discuss evaluation and assessment in more detail.

7. Bibliography Select a bibliography, including the following:
    a. books to be read by students
    b. books that might be read to the students
    c. poems that might be part of the unit
    d. teachers' references
    e. instructional materials: journals, reproductions of paintings, audio-visual materials, Internet connections, possible outside speakers, and field trips

Is this the only way a unit can be created? Of course not. Also, this model works for disciplinary and interdisciplinary units as well as integral units. If you examine the steps above, you will discover that nothing will be different for a disciplinary unit except that the activities will reflect only one discipline. Since that is true, it is likely that you will need a shorter block of time to teach a disciplinary unit than an integral unit. Whether you teach through integral, disciplinary, or interdisciplinary units, this kind of careful planning is necessary.

Those who have never planned or taught an integral unit may wonder what the activities might look like. The possibilities are limitless, but an example may be helpful. Ryan Gritter and other teachers at Westminster Christian School in Miami, Florida, planned a basketball project that their eighth-grade students have enjoyed. This exciting, worthwhile activity incorporates a knowledge of mathematics, geography, political science, art, and physical education:

Basketball Project

The students are required to write a three-page paper in which they act as a manager for a U.S. basketball team.

Page 1: This is the cover page containing the student's name, the name of the team, and any illustrations the student chooses to include.

Page 2: The student charts the twenty games the team will play, giving the date, the opponent, the city where the game will be played, the latitude and longitude of the city, the distance from the site of the last game, and the type of government of that country.

Page 3: This is a world map where the student traces the path of the team's trip.

Requirements:
1. The total distance of travel must be under 25,000 miles.
2. The team must play ten games in the United States and ten games in other countries.
3. Games played in other countries must be played in the capital city.
4. The team may not play in any city twice.

Chapter 5

> 5. The team may not play more than three games in a row on the same continent.
> 6. The team must play on at least four continents.
> 7. The team must play one game in a monarchy and one in a democracy other than the United States.

Students work independently and are given a little more than a week to complete the project. In school they work on the project during social studies and science classes. In art class the students use red, white, and blue paint to paint their team's t-shirt. They wear these t-shirts for the Field Day activities, which are the culminating point of the project. On Field Day the students are placed in four teams to play different basketball activities. For example, there is a "Round-the-World Shooting Contest," in which the teachers mark different spots on the court. Each team stands in a spot, and team members take turns shooting until one team member makes the shot. Then the team may advance to the next spot. The movie *Hoosiers* is also part of Field Day.

When it comes to planning middle school schedules, the single most important principle is that they must be flexible. Teachers need to be able to move freely from traditional blocks of time to longer blocks, depending on instructional needs. This can usually be arranged by giving a large block of time to the teacher team at any grade level and allowing them to arrange instructional blocks according to the instructional task. This kind of scheduling becomes difficult when high school teachers are brought in to teach middle school subjects, making at least that part of the schedule inflexible.

No two middle schools are alike, but we can learn much by examining what some schools have done. For example, Chairo Christian School in Druin, Australia, has made the care and development of the wetlands surrounding the school an important focus of their curriculum. Students study the soil, research the plants that flourish in that soil, work with plant propagation, and are actively involved in planting and caring for the area.

With the guidance of teachers, the students have built a waterfall on the grounds and are planning for a trout farm.

The academic year at Mount Evelyn Christian Middle School in Melbourne, Australia, is divided into four terms. In the first term students do a grade-specific unit. Grade 7 students explore aspects of personality, relationships, and body systems and changes, at all times focusing on the unity of the middle school person. Grade 8 students explore the changes and challenges people face as they move through adolescence toward adulthood, learning to take increasing responsibility for their time and lifestyle. Grade 9 students focus on the city of Melbourne, its history and development, life in the inner city and suburbs, and how the city functions.

For terms two, three, and four, the students move to multi-age integral units with seventh, eighth, and ninth graders in class together with teacher teams for each section. The integral unit topics are taught in a three-year cycle. Topics for these units include studies of how individuals and groups express themselves in ways that reflect God-given creativity, cultures and cultural expressions, planet Earth, different forms of communication, media, the integrality and interdependence of life in our natural environments, their own school life and how the school functions in the community, people's partnership with the land, and ways in which resources are distributed. In addition to the multi-age groups, students are involved in skill studies, which are taught in year-specific groupings to facilitate sequential skill development.

For Discussion

1. What is it that drives the curriculum in your school? To what extent do the textbooks determine what your students will study? Are you satisfied that the way curriculum is planned in your school provides the best possible education for your students?

2. What attitudes do you hope are being developed in your Christian middle school students?

3. Do you know which skills are being taught and maintained throughout your school?
4. What steps should your group of teachers take to ensure that the best possible learning is taking place in your middle school?

References

Caine, Renate and Geoffrey Caine. *Education on the Edge of Possibility*. Alexandria, VA: Association for Supervision and Curriculum Development. 1997.

Grene, Marjorie *Approaches to a Philosophical Biology*. NY: Basic Books, 1968.

Hirsch, E. D. *The Core Knowledge Series: Resource Books for Grades One Through Six.* New York: Del Publishing Co, 1993.

Jacobs, H. H. *Interdisciplinary Curriculum: Design and Implementation.* Alexandria, VA: Association for Supervision and Curriculum Development, 1989.

Stronks, Gloria Goris and Doug Blomberg. *A Vision with a Task: Education for Responsive Discipleship.* Grand Rapids, MI: Baker Book House, 1993.

Chapter 6

Finding Your Word in the Gospels
One Approach to Teaching
Eighth-Grade Bible

Several years ago I was told that in addition to teaching seventh- and eighth-grade English, I would be teaching eighth-grade Bible. During the summer vacation, I pored over the existing material, but its black-and-white, straightforward, strictly academic approach left me cold. Fortunately I have been blessed with a principal who encourages our creativity so long as we meet certain requirements and standards, and he allowed me to develop my own Bible curriculum, provided I covered the part of the Bible studied in eighth grade, which is the four Gospels.

My primary purpose in this chapter is to present an overview of what I have done for seven years now in eighth-grade Bible. The curriculum has grown each year, with new ideas coming as I delve into each Gospel, and of course I have deleted some things. But I have two additional motives for presenting this to you. One is to encourage you to develop your own curriculum if what you now use seems inadequate. Don't settle for someone else's material if it does not fit your vision, or your school's vision, for what should be taught. Developing curriculum takes time, but it is highly rewarding to present your students with what is really yours. There is something about ownership that instills confidence in a teacher. Another motive I have for presenting this material hinges on what I have just said. If you develop your own materials, particularly in Bible, you can offer students a "key" that will unlock the door to what you will be discovering together.

What do I mean by a key? To explain, I will describe my process in writing this Bible program. I had just finished reading Frederick Buechner's wonderful book *Wishful Thinking: A Theological ABC* (New York: Harper and Row, 1973), in which he takes single words that are significant to spiritual matters and addresses them. It occurred to me that an exciting way to approach the four Gospels would be to find strong spiritual words in each Gospel and have the students attempt to define them. And this became the key that unlocked what has become a spiritual journey for me and my students as we explore the Gospels together.

And so I began with the book of Matthew. As I read it with more eager eyes than ever before, I chose seven words I considered important to a valid approach to this Gospel:

- faith
- law/love
- grace
- sacrifice
- pride
- omnipresence

I begin my eighth-grade Bible class this way. I give all the students journals, and I tell them that the text for this course is their Bible, which they should be able to write in if they choose to. If a student does not have a Bible, our school has several cast-off copies, which I sell them for one dollar. I give a brief overview of what we will be doing in the class, as well as the following guidelines for their journal writing:

1. Unless otherwise instructed, you must always write your answers in complete sentences.
2. Answers like "I don't know" or "I can't think of anything" are not acceptable. If you're struggling to understand or to come up with an answer, please feel free to ask me for help.
3. You may not work with anyone else when you answer these questions. They need to be *your* responses.

Chapter 6

4. Your definition of the word we are studying is one of the most important parts of your journaling. *Struggle* with it. Make it a definition that gives new insight into an old word.
5. The summaries you write at the end of our exploration of each word are important as well. I am looking for evidence that you are referring to specific things we did during our examination of that word.
6. For *all* questions that demand thought, avoid answering with "Sunday School" responses. I am looking for thoughtful honesty, which I may or may not agree with—either way, your grade will not reflect whether I agree but whether you gave the matter some serious pondering. In other words, do not crank out familiar, safe-sounding phrases.

And then we begin a study of our first word, *faith*. I bombard my students with various ways of exploring this word. We read a short story that centers around faith. We look at Hebrews 11, the "heroes of faith" passage, explore what these heroes have in common, and come to some surprising conclusions. We listen to the song "That's What Faith Must Be," by Michael Card, and I read to them an article by Philip Yancey about "Old Faithful." There is a wonderful BC cartoon that deals with faith, and we respond to it together. Some of our responses are in our journals, and some are simply in discussion. Sometimes students find a quiet spot outside, where they write their summaries and their final definitions. Exploring one word may take three to five days. At the end, the students hand in their journals, and I grade them, rather subjectively at times. But, as I have said in my journal instructions, I grade them not according to how far they've gone in their spiritual journey, but according to the amount of struggle I see reflected in those pages.

Allow me to walk you through some specific word lessons. When we get to the word *omnipresent* in our study of "Matthew words," we do some fairly straightforward but rather unusual

Reaching and Teaching Young Adolescents

things. I read my students a small excerpt from C. S. Lewis' *The Horse and His Boy,* and they respond in their journals to such questions as these:
1. From the selection, list at least three qualities you saw in the lion (for example, he has warm breath). How are they qualities you would expect to find in someone good?
2. What does Aslan reveal to Shasta about the various lions he has met on his journey?
3. What is Aslan's response when Shasta asks, "Who *are* you?"
4. When Shasta can finally see Aslan, what is his response? Explain.
5. How is God's omnipresence comforting? How is it frightening?
6. Explain how the following passages support the idea that God is omnipresent:
   a. Psalm 139:7-12
   b. Jonah 1:1-17

After this we look at Psalm 139 together, and I ask my students to rewrite it, making it uniquely theirs. Here are some wonderful responses from students who are acknowledging and tracing their steps with God, as the psalmist did long ago:

Oh Lord, you know the exact second I will run out the door, even before I awaken. You knew I would raise my hand to answer that question in English. You knew every pencil mark I would make on my Conclusion assignment. You are with me every stroke of a paint brush on my painting in art class, and you are following every note I play on my cello. You know what song I will sing even before I will think of one. You surround me in all the things I choose to work at, even if I'm not very good at them. You hold me in your hand.

I cannot go anywhere and be away from you. Doing my homework, you are with me. Talking on the phone or baby-sitting those naughty kids next door, you are still with me. If I were to travel

Chapter 6

across the ocean to France or Germany or the many places I dream of, I will still never wander from your hand.

You know who I will marry, or even if I won't marry. I praise you because you made every inch of me. Even before I was loved by my parents, I was loved by you. You knew every blink of my eye and every wiggle of my fingers, even before they did. Why can't you not create people who murder and steal and do drugs? People like Jeffrey Dahmer, for instance. I know the answer—you love them too, and I sin like they do, only in different ways.

Come into my heart and memorize me some more. Take my life and mold it to fit what you desire.

Beautiful, isn't it? And then there's this one, done by a very creative person and an avid computer fan, which is pretty obvious as you watch his metaphor unfold:

Lord, You know everything about me because you have given me a complete scan for viruses. Whether it's via satellite or something else, you know every single move I make, and even know when I will do it. . . .

You did a great job designing me at the factory, with the highest quality workmanship, backed by a lifetime comprehensive warranty, and you did a terrific job. Thank you. You got on Microsoft Windows up there and used "Scheduler" to plan out my days before they would even happen. (You don't use Macs, do you?) And you don't even keep me minimized. All your windows up there are active! Surely you will pull the plug on those who are wicked on America Online. They misuse your name in their chat rooms—how stupid they are! I despise those who despise you . . . those virus-contributors, too, are enemies to you—and me, O Lord.

So run SCANDISK on me and store all my contents in your vast RANDOM ACCESS MEMORY. Test my mind and heart for viruses. Sound the alarm and notify me through "Call Center" if you find those and other things you don't like, such as program errors and bad programs or bitmaps that dishonor you, O Lord . . . and keep my system operating the way it was built to be.

Reaching and Teaching Young Adolescents

Finally, before we get to the summary and definition, I show a familiar cartoon about Pepe Le Peu, a skunk who is enthralled with a cat. I tell the students that the skunk's unwavering pursuit of the cat is much like God's inescapable presence as described in Psalm 139. It's also like the experience of the speaker in the poem "The Hound of Heaven," by Francis Thompson. I ask them to list in their journals things the skunk says that remind them of what God might be saying to us, and the cat's response, which might be the way we sometimes respond to God's pursuit of us. We have a wonderful discussion on this.

And then come the summary and the definition. Let me share one summary and two definitions with you:

Summary:

God's omnipresence is like a golden crown encompassing our world like another protective layer of our atmosphere. But this presence is not just confined to earth. He fills the universe, and heaven too. His ever-present, holy breath seems to come from nowhere, but it fills our lungs, so that we have to call out to him. Even though we might think God is trying to get too involved or even hurt us or interfere, he is simply helping us on our journey, watching us as we write our story. When we finally see him at certain amazing moments, we are ashamed that we did not trust him. We foolishly pant and panic as we run away from him, only to realize that we cannot rest until we rest in his loving arms. He is always tirelessly pursuing us, and sooner or later we surrender. Then we have peace.

Definitions:

Omnipresence means that God is my shadow, and the sun is always shining.

Omnipresence means that if you go to someone's house, God is already there to answer the door . . . if you go to the woods, God has made a path for you . . . and if you go to a campfire at the end of the day, God already has the fire going, and a bag of marshmallows ready.

Chapter 6

When we have completed our study of all the words that play an important role in Matthew, we go to the book of Matthew itself, and we spend two to three weeks looking at how those words shape this Gospel. So, for example, if we have been looking at *law/love,* we consider the Pharisees, and we see what they are missing and what Jesus is offering them. And we hear in new tones Jesus' compelling words: "I have not come to abolish the law, but to fulfill it." We study the parables (and sometimes tell or dramatize them) in the light of *faith* and *grace* and *sacrifice*. And we see the power of Jesus' promise of His *omnipresence* at the end of Matthew's Gospel when he says, "Lo, I am with you always, even to the end of the world." *And because students have claimed and explored and defined these words for themselves, they understand better.*

Mark's gospel has five key words:
- fear (including holy fear)
- evil
- baptism
- miracle
- hope

And once again, we begin exploring these words in a variety of ways. When we have finished, we study the book of Mark, discovering how these words are important to the person Mark, who is telling his version of the story of Jesus.

Then we look at Luke's words:
- joy
- prayer
- forgiveness
- image of God
- mercy

I have mentioned in previous chapters the importance of not only studying *about* spiritual truths as they are presented in the Bible, but also attempting to *approach* God in worship as we study. Of course, the word *prayer* allows this to happen. During our study of prayer, we also pray. Here are some other things we do:

Knol

Reaching and Teaching Young Adolescents

We watch a video clip of the movie *Sarafina*—the opening scene, in which the South African school is burning down and the teacher is asked to lead the students in morning prayers. "The Lord's Prayer" is then sung and danced to in a glorious, celebratory manner. I have a friend who teaches dance, and I asked her to help us learn at least a modified version of that "Sarafina dance." I think we prayed as we danced it. Two students act out a simple skit on prayer, involving God's response to someone's prayers. It is both poignant and amusing. *Life* magazine ran an article called "Why We Pray," in which people of all walks of life and various ages were interviewed. I read the article and ask the students to list in their journals truths and untruths about prayer that they gleaned from the responses. Then we discuss them. We learn how to sign the Lord's Prayer for the hearing impaired. And I also ask my students to draw in their journals what prayer looks like. These drawings need not be detailed, but they are insightful testimonies of what prayer means to the students.

Chapter 6

Summary

Prayer is when we ask God to do what we can't, or it is a time to thank Him. We humans see life through a curtain most of the time; through prayer, God lifts that curtain so that we can see things as they really are. Prayer is also having faith and not giving up, even if no answers come right away . . . you keep knocking until Someone comes, even if it takes you a lifetime. Some people believe they are in control, so they don't need prayer, but we need to believe that we must come to God and allow Him control. Prayer is not something you say because you were taught to do so since you were a little kid. You don't pray out of duty or habit, saying the same things without meaning them. Prayer is a sincere conversation with God, telling Him about what has happened that day, what you feel you need help with, or just stopping to say thanks. When you take the time to confess in your talk with God, you feel the load on your chest lifted. Finally, the position of prayer does not have to be on your knees, although it can be. If you are silent and speak through signing, or if you dance before God, you can have a blast spending time with Him.

Definitions:
Prayer is having a cup of tea with an old friend.

Prayer is turning the doorknob to the room where God lives.

And finally, we come to the book of John. I think you can see why our study of the Gospels takes an entire school year.

These are the words for John:
- truth
- peace
- holiness
- remember

One of my favorite words comes in this part of the curriculum. It is the word *holiness*. I think students already have a strong inward sense of the meaning of the word *holy*, but they may not have been able to name it as such. As we begin our study, I ask them to tell about a "holy moment" they remember. The

Chapter 6

responses are fascinating! As you can imagine, many students describe times when they were awed by God's majesty and this brought them to natural praise. But others talk about times of suffering when they found themselves experiencing God's comfort in ways they hadn't known before. And still others mention moments alone in bed at night. As they were sorting through the events of their day, it suddenly occurred to them that God was involved in those events. It is interesting that their holy moments are rarely in church. Perhaps they omit this because it seems too obvious. I hope this is the case. However, I think it may also indicate that middle school students rarely find in church any opportunity to experience God at their level of understanding.

We look at God's holiness through stories in the Bible where in our eyes He seems to "over-react"—the story of Uzzah, struck dead when the ark slipped off the cart, or the story of Ananias and Sapphira, struck dead for lying to Peter. And we look at the very end of the movie *Raiders of the Lost Ark*, when almost everyone is destroyed as the ark of the covenant is opened. And we talk about how God's holiness is both "awe-ful" and "awesome." And then, once again, students are asked to draw . . . what does holiness look like?

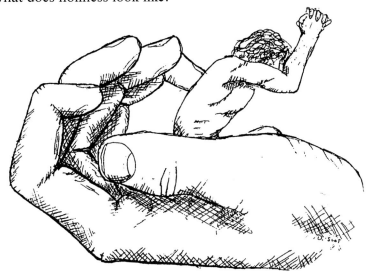

After this, as usual, the students write a summary based on these and a few other encounters, and again they attempt to write a simple definition out of their own understanding and, hopefully, their own hearts.

We end the school year with a study of John's Gospel from the perspective of the powerful words we have just studied. Allow me to close this chapter with a few more random definitions and a student's comments on his eighth-grade Bible experience. First, the definitions:

Grace is God loving me just because.
Grace is a flower blooming in infertile soil.
Grace is God letting you cut in line.

Hope is the Love that has yet to find us.
Wishing has an element of fairy tale in it—we wish upon a star;
    but hope is more of a sure thing—we hope towards a promise.
Hope is an open window.

Fear is allowing someone to pull the shades down so that you
    cannot see God at work.
Fear is the scratch in your soul that keeps you from success.

Evil is what keeps your head underwater when you are trying to
    inhale a breath of fresh air.

The image of God is a mirror. When you look into it, the reflection
    is one of what you are by grace—beautiful.
Image of God: a perfect Artist sitting on a stool in front of a mirror,
    dipping His paintbrush into rare colors and taking a deep
    breath.

Law is following the footsteps of your Father precisely in the beach
    sand, but Love is dancing over the sand.

Pride is taking down a portrait of someone and hanging up a larger
    one of yourself.

Chapter 6

Pride is committing eternal murder on two people—you and the other guy.
Pride is carefully placing yourself on a pedestal and enjoying the view.
Pride is a paper covered with glitter that is not glued on.

Sacrifice is disabling yourself so that someone else can fly.
Sacrifice is loving someone else more.

Miracle is a glimpse of God through a cardboard kaleidoscope.

Mercy is giving someone permission to try again.

Joy is holy happiness.

Heaven: Soul Garden

And here are one student's words as the class ended:

I have never taken Bible before. I loved it. I loved the worship times with candles, and the washing of feet, and the songs and videos and stories. I felt like I had found the family of God, and we were finding out what he had to say to us through the Bible and a whole lot more. I have gotten closer to God now, and I want to continue.

Reaching and Teaching Young Adolescents

Chapter 7
Teaching Responsive Discipleship
Assessment and Three-Way Conferences

> I feel that I do a good job of teaching except for every ninth week when report cards are due. Each time I am required to put grades on the report cards I go through the same excruciating pain. Of course I could do as many other teachers do and simply average the grades each student has earned during the grading period. But to me that seems so unfair. Do we evaluate their learning based on how many tries it took them to learn something? There are some students who, with very little effort, have earned a B average. There are others who need to work extremely hard simply to keep from failing. I don't know whether the problem is with me or with the system, but my instinct is that something is very wrong. I have asked the more experienced teachers to help me, but they say they don't have any better answers and that I will just have to harden myself to the grim fact that grades are needed. Hearing them talk makes me suspect that every teacher here would say that giving grades is necessary but is the hardest part of being a middle school teacher.

The speaker, who was nearing the end of a successful first year of teaching, had identified one of the most difficult parts of teaching at any level. That is the task of considering and making judgments about the learning a student has accomplished.

In the 1990s, assessment has emerged as an important part of schooling. One hears about "authentic assessment," and "assessment alternatives," and "performance assessment." The word *assessment* is derived from a Latin word meaning "to sit alongside and consider," and if we think about it that way, it should not be so difficult. The teacher and student sit together to consider what the student has learned. However, the task of assessing and grading remains one of the least comfortable and most talked about parts of a teacher's work.

Assessment takes many forms. Here are some examples:
- The students take a test to determine how much they learned from a unit of study.
- Students take a standardized achievement test.
- The teacher writes comments to accompany the report card.
- The teacher reads a student's learning log and decides whether he/she needs more instruction.
- The student keeps a portfolio of completed work and discusses its contents with parents and teacher in a conference.
- The student, teacher, and parents have a teacher-led discussion of the student's academic progress and social behavior.
- The student, teacher, and parents have a student-led discussion of the student's academic progress and social behavior.
- A team of teachers discuss a student's academic performance.
- Students, working in a cooperative group, critique one another's work.
- The teacher walks around and observes the students while they study to determine their study behaviors and their use of study skills.
- The student and teacher discuss the student's use of study skills.
- The teacher keeps anecdotal records of a student's class participation, behavior, and academic progress.
- A student creates an exhibit to demonstrate learning in a specific unit or discipline, and invites others to view the exhibit.
- Three students invite their parents and friends to an evening in which they each introduce and read poetry from a selected poet.

Underlying any discussion of how assessment should be done is a view of learning and teaching held by teachers, a view that may or may not be reflected in the school's mission statement. Is the role of the teacher that of a judge who decides what

Chapter 7

students have passed and failed and who determines what grades they have earned? Should it be the teacher's role to rank the class members so that students, parents, and future schools know the student's exact place in that ranking scheme? Is the teacher's role that of an encourager who provides only positive responses, believing one should "catch them doing well"? Should the teacher be a standard-bearer with a standard so high that all students are reminded that on earth we cannot be perfect and that imperfections must always be found and pointed out? Or given what we now know about learning, is the teacher's role different from any of these?

Why We Assess

We believe that assessment is a vital part of learning for the following reasons:

1. We assess in order that the student will think about his own learning strengths and weaknesses. Through assessment, we hope to help students understand to what extent they have successfully fulfilled their responsibilities.
2. We assess so that the teacher may determine how much a student knows about a body of material in order to plan future instruction. Thus, in courses with content that is sequential, students will not move forward until they have been successful at each level.
3. We assess in order to motivate students to study and to direct them toward better ways of studying.
4. We assess in order to communicate to the student and parents how well the student is learning or behaving.
5. We assess so that administrators, board members, and parents can be comfortable in the knowledge that students are learning in ways that are in keeping with the school's mission statement.

Problems with Assessment

When teachers assess using only standardized tests and traditional teacher-made tests, they reflect a view of learning that is prevalent everywhere but that we now know is simply not true. The following assumptions, stated earlier in chapter 5, underlie this view:
1. Only experts create knowledge.
2. Teachers deliver knowledge in the form of information.
3. Children are graded on how much of the information they have stored. (Caine and Caine, 1997, p. 60)

Teachers who hold such assumptions will view assessment as finding out how much content knowledge each student has stored. Both traditional standardized tests and many teacher-made tests are geared toward assessing stored knowledge. When I was a child in rural Minnesota, eighth graders were required to take "state boards," which were examinations in English, geography, science, and mathematics. I scored well on those state boards because the teacher gave us a great deal of material to memorize in preparation for the tests, and memorizing information was easy for me. Years later I looked back at my copies of those tests and realized that, as an eighth-grade student, I had understood very little of that information. Nor had I retained much of it.

In a book that teachers in every Christian middle school should read and discuss, *Education on the Edge of Possibility,* Caine and Caine (1997) explain that we have an idea that learning always occurs in a linear fashion and is always cause and effect: if we teach this, that will happen. School restructuring efforts along with debates about national standards echo this belief and advocate more time for the same, more effort for the same, more strategies—and yet the results are disappointing. A great deal of activity is going on to change the schools, but that activity will be counterproductive so long as the delivery of knowledge and assessment of learning remain the same.

Chapter 7

What We Know About Learning

Popular news-magazine articles on learning and the human brain show us that learning is far more complex than we have assumed. Both *Time* and *Newsweek* have run cover articles on the topic. We know, for example, that our minds are more than what our brain does. Researchers into the way minds and bodies work believe that intelligence is in every cell of the body and that mind is not confined to the space above the neck but is found throughout the brain and the body (Moyers 1993, p. 183). Researchers such as Neal Miller (1995) and Marian Diamond (1988) tell us that the body, brain, and mind are connected so that when we choose to change our behavior, the chemistry of the brain changes too. In many ways our experiences shape our brains.

> We are suggesting the need to see that body, brain, and mind form a dynamic unity, the nature and possibilities of which far exceed, and are qualitatively different from, those of the constituent parts. To that end, we have a need to examine profound issues that go beyond brain research. How we interpret and use the research will have a much greater impact than the research itself. (Caine and Caine, 1997, p. 79)

We know that learning is grounded in a sense of wholeness, rather than fragmentation. It is not that we don't know enough about learning to change teaching and assessment. The truth is that we do not use what we know. Christians have answers to profound questions, and those answers should lead us to helping students become all that they were made to be.

There is evidence that changes are happening in some Christian middle schools. Del Brower, principal at Community Christian School in Willmar, Minnesota, said, "We had our seventh graders explain to their parents on parent night what activities they were doing in school and what they were learning. The parents were excited about the students' eagerness to be involved. The teachers were thrilled to see how much it meant to students." What those students were doing on that parent night is part of the assessment of real learning.

We need to ask ourselves, How would assessment change if we truly believed that learning is the acquisition of *meaningful* knowledge instead of the delivery of information supplied by experts? Assessment in this light takes the form of a teacher and student monitoring learning together rather than the teacher simply judging what and how much the student has learned.

What We Mean by Authentic Assessment

When we assess learning, we gather evidence of what a student can do. Next, we evaluate the student's learning by interpreting that evidence and basing decisions on it. Our assessment needs to be ongoing and frequent so that we can make instructional decisions based on the evidence.

Assessment that serves as an alternative to traditional multiple-choice, standardized achievement tests or traditional teacher-made tests is often called "authentic assessment." Authentic assessment provides information about specific tasks that the student can or cannot do, but those tasks must be worthwhile, significant, and meaningful. Tom Stefonek (1991) gives us the following definitions and phrases identified with experts who call for authentic assessment:

- Methods that emphasize learning and thinking, especially higher-order thinking skills such as problem-solving strategies (Collins)
- Tasks that focus on students' ability to produce a quality product or performance (Wiggins)
- Disciplined inquiry that integrates and produces knowledge, rather than reproducing fragments of information others have discovered (Newmann)
- Meaningful tasks at which students should learn to excel (Wiggins)
- Challenges that require knowledge in good use and good judgment (Wiggins)
- A new type of positive interaction between the assessor and assessee (Wiggins)

- An examination of differences between trivial school tasks (e.g., giving definitions of biological terms) and more meaningful performance in nonschool settings (e.g., completing a field survey of wildlife) (Newmann)
- Involvement that demystifies tasks and standards (Wiggins) (Found in Burke, 1994, pp. 8-9)

When middle school teachers assess student learning, they should gather as much information as possible across different settings and times. The information should come from a variety of sources such as formal and informal tests, observations, checklists, contracts, rubrics, work sampling, exhibits, and portfolios.

Rubrics are clear criteria set forth in advance so that students and teacher can see what kinds of performance are acceptable and what kinds are not. Mary Beth Horton, a middle school teacher at Westminster Christian School in Miami, says that one of her greatest frustrations has been developing a good system for evaluating creative writing assignments fairly. She now shares with her students the following rubric by which their writing is evaluated:

1. Is there a correct heading?
2. Does every sentence begin with a capital letter?
3. Does every sentence end with appropriate punctuation?
4. Is there an effective topic sentence?
5. Is there an appropriate "clincher" sentence?
6. Are there three or more supporting details?
7. Is your paper "teacher friendly"?
8. Is there a variety of sentences?
9. Are there transitional words?
10. Is the purpose of the paper clear?

She shares with her students exactly how each area is weighted so that the students will know the basis for their grades.

In *work sampling* the teacher keeps a file of a student's work in specific categories, gathered at different times in the year. After collecting the data, the teacher carefully examines it and makes an evaluation or judgment of the student's learning.

These days we recognize the importance of encouraging students to gather data concerning their own learning, and they often do so by means of portfolios. A *portfolio* is a student's organized collection of her work, gathered thoughtfully over a specific time period. It may contain samples of both finished work and work in progress, including journal entries, drawings, audio- and videotapes, photographs, and other appropriate products. Together the teacher and student evaluate the student's learning by looking at what she has done and by examining the changes in her products over time. Above all, assessment must be thoughtful and have thoughtful outcomes if it is to lead to the instruction students need next.

Traditional Test-Taking

Standardized achievement tests have an important role, provided they reflect instructional content that is actually taught in that school. Their results inform the school administrator and parents concerning how the school compares with other schools.

However, standardized achievement tests do not provide accurate and adequate information about how one particular student compares with the rest of the class because there are too many variables. Teachers recognize that variables which keep students from performing well on a standardized test include the following: the student may not be physically well on the testing day, the student may have experienced an emotional upheaval just before the test, or the student may not be good at taking such tests. Sometimes a student will perform much better than one would expect, given his class performance. A standardized test tells teachers very little about the achievement of individual students but can tell the administrator and parents something about how learning in that school compares with learning in other schools. When too much reliance is placed on standardized test performance, the student may get a distorted view of what learning actually is and also may be classified inappropriately.

Well-constructed teacher-made content tests are another important element in school assessment. The results of such tests tell the teacher which students have gained certain information or skills and which ones need further instruction.

The teachers of the Grand Rapids Christian School Association use the following chart to help themselves think about assessment in broader terms and to help them evaluate their own success with assessing in a variety of ways:

Assessment Watching

How is learning assessed in your classroom? Be on the lookout for methods of assessment that measure one or more of the following. Briefly describe the context and the assessment. Some of these will happen very quickly: i.e., a show of hands in response to a question. Watch for subtle, unique ways of assessing.

Perceptions: attitude/opinion survey, self-assessment, goal-setting, prior knowledge check

Processes: draft-writing, lab work, problem-solving research, planning, strategizing, use of skills taught, learning log, ability to work cooperatively in a group, organization, time management

Performances: tests, projects, final draft writing, artwork, class presentations, demonstrations, reader's theater, plays, spreadsheets, graphic organizers

Proficiency: What records are kept, or what evidence is saved, that shows the individual learner's growth? This includes the results of standardized tests.

—Boehm, 1998

Three-Way Conferences

To help students learn responsive discipleship by taking responsibility for their own work and for the learning, care, and nurture of classmates, many schools are finding the three-way conference extremely worthwhile. Such conferences—with student, parents, and teacher—follow one of three patterns: teacher-led conferences, student-led conferences, and student-parent conferences with the teacher present in the room but not attending the conference. Some schools have tried all three, while others have chosen a particular way of conferencing because they have found it the most beneficial.

The purpose of the three-way conference is to involve the student directly in the evaluation of his performance and behavior. When only the teacher and parents are present, the students know they are the topic of conversation. When parents return from the conference with any request for better behavior or more careful academic work, students are often quick to try to justify their own actions and find fault with the school. If it is the student whose behavior or performance we are addressing and hoping to change, surely that student ought to be present at the discussion.

However the conference is set up, students must be prepared for what will happen there. If they are to lead the discussion, they must learn how. If the teacher is to lead, the students should know in advance what matters will be discussed and how they will fare in those matters.

On the very first day at Sylvan Christian School, the eighth-grade teachers tell their classes that students will lead the three-way conference to take place in November. They promise the students that, when the time comes, they will be prepared to do so. The teachers then role-play for the students (rather hilariously, say the students) things that should *not* happen in a conference. All through September and October students keep portfolios of their work. As conference time draws near, students select from their portfolios work that they think best represents their learning during that time. Students discuss their progress and behavior with their teachers so that they will know how to approach the topics during the conference. Then there is a great deal of student role-playing to help them be as comfortable as possible while they are leading the conference. Parents report that they are very impressed, pleased, and even surprised

Chapter 7

to see their children demonstrate such confidence and ability to assess their own work. Parents and teachers recognize the importance of these conferences in helping students learn to take responsibility for their own learning and behavior.

Teachers use three-way conferences in Christian middle schools in many parts of North America. The teachers who do so say it takes a great deal of effort to prepare students for a conference, but the learning that results is so important that such conferences should be held in every middle school grade at least once each year.

Excellent books have been written about ways of assessing in middle schools. For suggestions on authentic assessment, the following are particularly helpful: *How to Assess Authentic Learning* by K. Burke (1994), *Authentic Reading Assessment* by Valencia, Hiebert, and Afflerbach (1994), and *A Practical Guide to Alternative Assessment* by Herman, Aschbacher, and Winters (1992). These three books offer excellent ideas for portfolios, performances and exhibitions, projects, learning logs and journals, metacognitive reflection strategies, and observation checklists.

We've come a long way since the days of assigning grades on the basis of multiple-choice tests, quizzes, and worksheets. As responsive disciples of Jesus Christ, middle school students must learn to monitor their own learning so that they can act responsibly toward themselves and others. We can help them do so through the way we plan assessment.

For Discussion

1. When you examine your own teaching using the chart prepared by Norma Boehm, how do you fare? Do you have appropriate examples in each area? Should you?
2. Do the standardized tests used in your school really reflect the instructional content and skills you are emphasizing?
3. What kinds of performances, exhibitions, and portfolios are appropriate for your middle school?

References

Boehm, Norma. Personal correspondence, 1998.

Burke, Kay *The Mindful School: How to Assess Authentic Learning.* Palatine, IL: IRI/Skylight Publishing, 1994.

Caine, Renate and Geoffrey Caine, *Educating on the Edge of Possibility.* Alexandria, VA: Association for Supervision and Curriculum Development, 1997.

Diamond, Marian. *Enriching Heredity: The Impact of the Environment on the Anatomy of the Brain.* New York: The Free Press, 1988.

Herman, Joan, Pamela Aschbacher, and Lynn Winters. *A Practical Guide to Alternative Assessment.* Alexandria, VA: ASCD, 1992.

Miller, Neal E., "Clinical Experimental Interactions in the Development of Neuroscience." *American Psychologist* 50 (1995): 901–911.

Moyers, Bill. *Healing and the Mind.* New York: Doubleday, 1993.

Stefonek, Tom. *Alternative Assessment: A National Perspective:* Policy Briefs No. 15 and 16. Oak Brook, IL: North Central Regional Educational Laboratory, 1991.

Valencia, Sheila, Elfrieda Hiebert, and Peter Afflerbach. *Authentic Reading Assessment: Practices and Possibilities.* Newark, Delaware: International Reading Association, 1994.

Chapter 8

"Panting, He Purchased the Pearl"
Worship in the Christian Middle School

I am about to confess something that has been a secret until now between me and another teacher. It occurs to me, as I write, that I have been foolish to keep it quiet because it is an important and holy event that we have guarded so closely. On the other hand, I am hesitant to share it for fear it will be misunderstood. Here is the secret. Each year before school begins, another teacher and I find time at the school building alone. We bring a small vial of oil with us, and we anoint all the doors of the school building. At each door, we pray specifically about those who will pass through, about all those who will be learning and growing in the room behind that door. We've carried on this tradition for three years now, and I must say that in those three years I have felt more protected and more successful than ever before.

I do not bring this to you as a kind of magic formula for a spiritual school. When I say successful, I mean that I have had a clearer understanding of how to approach the difficulties that every school year brings. I should add that in the last three years we have had terrible tragedies and obstacles at our school. A student died from drowning. A student was checked into a mental hospital. Families are struggling more than ever with abuse and divorce. Several staff members have had to face personal illness and the death of loved ones. It has been a hard three years, but we have been strong and beautiful through it. And I attribute this, in part, to our beginning the year in recognition of our need for God's blessing and strength and presence.

Here are some things you may or may not know about anointing. In Old Testament times both people and objects were anointed to emphasize their holiness and separation as God's material for His use. Anointing was man acting on God's behalf, signifying God's favor. Furthermore, it was a way of equipping for the service of God, and many passages in the Bible suggest that God's Spirit is poured out with the oil. So a king was anointed with oil, and the people knew that this was someone chosen by God, usually through the voice of the prophet. But soldiers were also anointed with oil as a way of preparing them for battle. In the New Testament, this idea was carried further when elders anointed the sick with oil, seemingly as a way of calling on God to give life and to equip through His Spirit.

Our time of anointing feels like worship. We call on God to cover this place with His Spirit because we feel inadequate to serve without Him. We know that we in Christian education are in a battlefield, and we want Him to prepare us.

How does one promote and encourage spirituality in middle school? This question is hard to answer, and yet it is at the heart of what we are called to offer our students. I'll simply relate in this chapter some obvious and not-so-obvious avenues I have seen in our school that have drawn out a positive response to the calling of God on young hearts.

In his fascinating book *Surprised by Joy*, C. S. Lewis describes the loss of his faith. Interestingly, it happened at age thirteen, and he attributes it, at least in part, to a teacher. It was not that she consciously set out to destroy his faith. But because she was not a Christian, her framework loosened his framework and in his words, "blunted all the sharp edges of my belief." Lewis says he was ripe for surrendering his faith at this time because he was feeling rather despairing about the state of the world anyway:

> There was ingrained in me a kind of pessimism, a pessimism much more of intellect than of temper. I was now by no means unhappy, but I had definitely formed the opinion that the universe was, in the main, a rather regrettable institution. There are some that will laugh at the idea of a loutish, well-fed young boy . . . passing an unfavorable judgment on the cosmos. . . . *They are forgetting what boyhood felt like from within.*

Chapter 8

> Dates are not so important as people believe. *I fancy that most of those who think at all have done a great deal of their thinking in the first fourteen years.* . . . Perhaps I had better call all this a settled expectation that everything would do what you did not want it to do. Whatever you wanted to remain straight would bend; whatever you tried to bend would fly back to the straight; all knots which you wished to be firm would come untied; all knots you wanted to untie would remain firm. It is not possible to put it into language without making it comic, and I have indeed no wish to see it (now) except as something comic. *But it is perhaps just these early experiences which are so fugitive and, to an adult, so grotesque, that give the mind its earliest bias, its habitual sense of what is or is not plausible.* [Emphasis mine]

In leading children of middle school age into worship, or in teaching them about God, we must be aware of the poignant truths Lewis points to here. Middle school students are generally sad about the state of the world. I mean the world both in the cosmic sense and in the more personal sense of their own experience in the cosmos thus far. I cannot tell you how many times I have heard or read student comments about what a sorry state the world is in. This comes from their concern—a much greater concern, I must say, than I had at the same age—about violent crime, pollution, divorce, and lack of integrity in government. It also comes from their frustration with themselves, even over something as simple and natural as their own clumsiness physically or socially. To surrender oneself in worship to God seems absurd. First, you might look foolish. And second, buried way down is the compelling question of why God would even *want* you on His side. There is a remarkable paradox in the minds and hearts of middle schoolers. On the one hand, far too often they feel ugly, stupid, and worthless. On the other hand, they are self-absorbed and self-proclaiming. So the soil of their souls looks hard and forbidding, but in cultivating it, one will find the richest, most beautiful soil one could ever hope for.

But how to cultivate? Ah, that is the question. . . .

My experience in teaching and in life has been that worship comes in predictable and unpredictable forms, at likely and not-so-likely moments. Let me begin by addressing some of the obvious forms of worship in a Christian school. Morning devotions is a time set into our school schedule at the beginning of every day. We have fifteen minutes with our homerooms to attend to any necessary business and to start the day with prayer and perhaps a passage read from the Bible or some other devotional book. This can be a mundane, routine exercise, or it can set the tone for the entire day, for both the teacher and the students. One of my cardinal rules in morning devotions is *not* to require students to lead. I certainly offer the opportunity at any time, but *requiring* them to do so seems artificial and even presumptuous. Where is this student in relationship to God? Will he or she be reading without sincerity or desire? Then it is a futile exercise. You can't give what you don't have.

I begin the school year by inviting my students to lead in devotions, but I tell them they will never be required to do so. Now of course this leaves it up to the teacher to come prepared each day—but so be it. And don't think that students will never take you up on the offer, because they will. Someone finds a great song she wants everyone to hear, and she shares a few words on why it touched her. Someone reads something in his own personal devotions that he thinks should be shared with his peers. Such moments are genuine and beautiful. And because it is something *they* have requested, you can be sure their peers are curious and listening.

One can use a variety of activities in devotions. Perhaps the key word is *variety*. Sometimes I simply read a passage from the Bible and talk about how it spoke to me that day or at some significant moment in my life. Sometimes I read a story, a specifically spiritual story or one that is not spiritual in intent but has a small truth (NOT a moral!) for the day. One of my favorite examples is a story by Arnold Lobel, one of his famous *Frog and Toad* stories. In it, Frog has a dream about being the "star" on stage, and each time he shows off and proclaims himself, Toad grows a little smaller. I then play a song by Rebecca St. James called "You Then Me." Sometimes I teach my students a song in sign language. We also use "prayer cards" during devotions. Students express a need that we pray about, and afterwards they may choose to write the prayer request on a card that is then stapled to a bulletin board. If other students want to commit themselves to pray about that concern, they sign their initials to the card. Later, the student who requested the prayer may come back with a "progress report." On Fridays we have a special prayer devotional time, where one student makes a request or speaks of something she is thankful for, and then another student volunteers to make that part of the prayer time. In this way, we claim each other's petitions and praises, and we become more of a community. Once on Ascension Day I splurged and bought twenty-four helium balloons, all gold, and brought them to devotions. Then I read Madeleine L'Engle's poem "Ascension," in which she uses the wonderful image of a child letting go of a balloon and watching with longing as it soars away as a metaphor for what Christ's disciples must have felt as they watched His departure. We went outside to where we have three large crosses "planted," and in silence we released our balloons, along with silent prayers.

On Tuesdays our middle school students gather downstairs to hold chapel in a large basement-like room with a cement floor, chipped walls, disintegrating ceiling tiles, and visible pipes. One eighth grader wrote about this unlikely worship place in a poem:

Basement

The once cold and bitter cement floor
now glows and invites with His presence,
bold and strong beams of truth
support the crumbling, holy ceiling.
These now gentle, firm walls embrace
open hearts, tender tears, raised hands,
and forgiveness.
This is His house?

This is His house.

Each week a middle school staff member prepares the school's twenty-minute chapel time. We all have a turn, and consequently worship has a different "flavor" each week. One teacher may know someone in the community who can offer a meaningful word. Another teacher may choose to give his own testimony. I will never forget one teacher who spoke on the "right to life" issue. She told the story of a woman who was unable to have children but desperately wanted a child of her own. In a parallel part of the story, a woman who was unmarried and pregnant was seriously considering abortion. Predictably, the child was spared, and the first woman rejoiced in the gift of her adopted daughter. Unpredictably, the teacher revealed that *she* was that daughter.

And we have encouraged and cultivated student involvement in our chapels. Middle schoolers have danced, or acted out a small drama, or even given their own testimony. The point is that if worship time is made an integral part of the school day, the students will be interested and involved. Within each one of us there is a longing to approach God, and I often think that longing is especially strong at middle school age. So let us learn from one another about how to approach Him, and let us put time and energy and passion into making this time holy. Our bleak basement chapel has become holy ground for us, and we eagerly anticipate our chapel day.

Now I will proceed to some less likely worship territory. Every good Christian school teacher has been told that our faith must be integrated into all our students' learning, not simply our Bible or religion classes, and I feel this often happens. But worship is different from instruction, is it not? We can become informed about how God made our universe in a science class, but can we also find time to worship God as a *response* to that information? Some would say that this can be done privately later, but I think we neglect an important aspect of our Christian education vision if we hold too rigidly to that view. Let me give an example or two.

Chapter 8

I have a friend who teaches seventh-grade science, including astronomy. Her students become familiar with new discoveries and learn new terminology as they study the solar system and the Milky Way and black holes. And when she has finished teaching them, she uses a ribbon to illustrate what she has learned about how amazing God is. She uses a small part of the ribbon to show how much we know about the solar system. She shows how much, according to scientists, is yet to be discovered by unrolling yards and yards more ribbon. Then she quotes Isaiah 41:26, "Lift your eyes and look to the heavens: Who created all these? He who brings out the starry host one by one, and calls them each by name. Because of His great power and mighty strength, not one of them is missing." There is a moment of worship that occurs here when she goes beyond imparting knowledge to paying honor.

In Bible class we study Paul's letter to the Galatians. We look at the fruit-of-the-Spirit passage (Galatians 5:22-23), and perhaps we spend some time there in our discussion. Is there an opportunity for worship in this study? Of course. One teacher I know wrote in calligraphy the names of the nine fruits of the Spirit on nine separate cards, and placed a candle before each one. She read a description of her perception of what each fruit meant, and after doing so, she lit the candle for that particular fruit. When she had finished, she gave all the students a small white candle and asked them to think about one particular fruit of the Spirit that they especially longed for at this point in their lives. Then one by one the students went forward and lighted their candles before the one they had chosen. The students sat with their candles lit, and no one dripped wax intentionally, or played with the flame, or made inappropriate comments. They prayed quietly for the Spirit to give them the gift they had asked for, and I believe Paul's message came alive in that classroom.

Two years ago, I entered the main office just before school started. A young father, new in the area, was registering his child for kindergarten. I smiled at the little boy and greeted him, and then introduced myself to the father. The little boy tugged at my shirt and asked, "Are you a teacher?" I confirmed that I was and that I taught eighth graders. His expression immediately took on a look between indignation and fear as he shouted at his father, "*SEE*! I *TOLD* you there'd be big kids here!" And he burst into tears.

That got me thinking. Why should starting school be such a frightening prospect for this little boy? And what could I do about it? As a result, we began a program called "Prayer Partners" in which we paired eighth graders with kindergartners at the beginning of each year. About once a month my eighth graders would spend a class period doing some kind of activity with their prayer partners. Sometimes it involved putting a book together with them, or helping them write words, or reading a book to them. But we ended with some kind of worship, usually a time of prayer. One year we even taught them the sign language for the Lord's Prayer, which was an incredible blessing on both sides. Now these little ones had a "big buddy" who would watch out for them during recess times, and sometimes even sit with them on the bus! Sometimes the more unlikely the circumstances, the more beautiful the blessing.

Our graduation from middle school has become a time of worship. The students and their friends and relatives leave saying that it felt like a celebration of God's goodness. This result is accomplished through music and sometimes dance and prayer and carefully chosen words, and sometimes through sign language. But it is our calling as Christian school teachers to take such moments out of the arena of pomp and circumstance and reshape them as gatherings of God's covenant people.

In eighth-grade Bible I have a favorite assignment that I invariably give when we study Jesus' parables. Each student must rewrite a parable using alliteration. In other words, they must retell the parable, using as many words as they can that begin with the same sound. Remember the parable of the pearl of great price? Here are two of their alliterative versions of that incredible parable:

Chapter 8

> *The place where the Prince of Peace presides is partly like a perfectly profound peasant, peeking, pondering, and purchasing a precious pearl. Pending a pander, he peeked and picked up the precious pearl. Pondering how to pay for the perfect pearl, he packed his pickings and sold his pigs, pens, powder, pewter, paper, planes, pilots, and pesticides and paid for his perfectly profound pearl with passion.*
>
> *Persistently, the Place of Paradise is like a person peering patiently for a perfect pearl. Picking through the pile, the person picked a pearl of preposterous price. Painfully propelled away, he priced his possessions. People peered at them and paid. Panting, he purchased the pearl.*

That precious pearl, of course, is the kingdom of Jesus. We come to our students with all our knowledge and expertise and discipline and lesson plans and charm and wit. But in the end, it is the pearl that speaks to their longing. It is the pearl that draws them in. *Please prod precious young people to pant and perhaps to purchase through your own personal passion.*

For Discussion
1. What kind of worship experiences, likely and unlikely, happen in your middle school?
2. How can teachers be sensitized and prepared in leading students to God?
3. What has a student taught you lately about God?
4. What have you taught a student lately about God?

Appendix

Ideas from the Field

Middle School Ideas That Work

The following teaching ideas have been developed by individual teachers. If you would like more information concerning how they carried out their teaching strategies, you can write or call them. Their school addresses and telephone numbers are included.

> Chuck Muether, middle school language arts teacher, Pella Christian School, Pella, Iowa

Flexible-Space Classroom

I've always wanted to have a classroom structured so that students could be involved in a number of activities. Five years ago I borrowed an idea from a black box theater production I was directing. What I found so interesting about producing theater in a black box was that seating, lighting, and staging were completely flexible. If theater could be that flexible, what about the classroom? Mine was the smallest classroom in the junior high. Since desk arrangements were already restricted, I decided to build centers in the classroom using two abandoned spaces, the old furnace room and the coat rack area. I built a small, completely enclosed two-studio radio station. I installed battens and put up stage lights for a theater. And I created a writing center by reconditioning older IBM computers and forming a lab in the classroom. Now students can use the three centers as well as take part in regular teacher-directed instruction.

Eagle Radio

Many junior high English curricula include an oral communication unit in which students present traditional speeches. I did not want to replace the speech requirement, but I did want to supplement it with a learning activity that the students would value for its authenticity. With student assistance, we recycled old theater flats and created a makeshift studio out of the furnace room. We used a primitive PA system and installed speakers in the other classrooms. Students became excited at the idea of broadcasting a radio program to other classrooms, but their excitement died when teachers could not make a commitment to listen. With the help of grants and parent volunteers, we built a more permanent studio in the classroom, replete with an FCC-approved microtransmitter, so now students broadcast to the community. Their excitement is here to stay because this oral communication activity is real to them. Their programs are heard by an audience far larger than the teacher with the red pen.

Since part of the town could pick up our FM signal, we had to plan radio programs that would go beyond our own listening needs. We adopted a classical, choral, and light Christian contemporary format. Borrowing an idea from National Public Radio, we have created our own daily news program called "Hall Things Considered." Other student-invented programs include "Kinder Radio," for early elementary students; "Novella Aire," in which students read a classical novel; "Eagle Extra," a local sports-talk show; "Classical Connection" and "The Choral Tradition," both aimed at classical music lovers. Students may play their own Christian music during the "Christian Hit Radio" time slots.

When the seventh and eighth grade students first realized that they could reach an expanded audience, they asked how they could receive feedback. I was impressed by their desire for audience response, so I created rubrics for selected listeners. With the help of retired citizens, at-home moms, businesspeople, and teachers, I began to compile a weekly Eagle Radio staff bulletin. Students read comments from regular listeners and noted how their programs fared in the top 15 ratings. The downside of this media center is the extra preparation the teacher must do to keep the station on the air all day. But I have found that delegating the music programming and scheduling deejay shifts to responsible middle schoolers gives them a real sense of accomplishment. At school they record the news and create public-service announcements and promotional materials. To lessen the amount of preproduction recording, I set Monday aside as a production day for those who wish to record their programs rather than air them live.

The greatest reward in Eagle Radio comes as students discover the consequences of their actions. One example happened when three boys produced a sports show and incorporated background music as they read the scores and statistics. When the Eagle Radio staff bulletin was published, the students were surprised by the response of their listening audience. They learned that their choice of background music was offensive and not at all distinctively Christian. On a subsequent show, they apologized profusely and promised to be more discerning in their musical choices. To sum it up, these boys learned a lesson I could never have taught them.

The Newsroom

One of my favorites of the units I offer eighth graders is the Newsroom Unit. Basically, two separate eighth grade classes produce competing newscasts. The target audience is the seventh grade students, who watch videotaped newscasts and award modified Nielsen points based on newsworthiness, creativity, program unity, and Christian perspective. This unit so captivates students that I could take off for coffee and no one would notice.

The Major Motion Picture Unit

This isn't your regular "let's make a movie" unit. Seventh grade students undertake the roles of an entire production team (key grip, best boy, gaffer, and so forth). We write the script, act out roles, edit scenes, create special effects, and type and roll credits.

Reaching and Teaching Young Adolescents

Going Where No One Has Gone Before: The Sci-Fi and Space Unit

In conjunction with NASA's Challenger Learning Center, we simulate life on Mars in the classroom by building space colonies, communicating through wireless radios, and sending out space probes (students using those PE scooters) to the school's hallways. This unit is an integrative/ interdisciplinary study that includes science, math, history, art, and physical education.

Chuck Muether, Pella Christian Middle School, 216 Liberty Street, Pella, Iowa 50219-1763 Phone: 515-628-9506 Fax: 515-628-9506

Milt Van Drunen, Lansing Christian Middle School, Lansing, Illinois

History for Parents

When we study the Civil War or the Revolutionary War in seventh grade history class, we use the textbook material, but we also plan an evening program for parents and grandparents. We learn the war songs of the era, and we make hardtack. Students construct a simple musket to carry as they learn the basics of marching and drill. They prepare poster displays and oral presentations on such topics as weapons, medical treatment, food, important battles, activities of women in the war, and others.

Hobby Week

John Klompmaker, our Bible teacher, has developed a Hobby Week presentation. People from the community come to school to demonstrate their hobbies. Students discover ways that we Christians can use our time productively and creatively.

Milt Van Drunen or John Klompmaker, Lansing Christian Middle School, 3660 Randolph Street, Lansing, IL 60438. Phone: 708-474-1700 Fax: 708-474-1746

Appendix

Jeff Poppema, Community Christian School, Willmar, MN

Character Builders

I use a system that disciplines in a positive way. Students who misbehave get their names on the board as a warning. After that they receive a check behind their names, and they lose their recess privileges. They then get a "Character Builder" to fill out and have signed by their parents. As soon as it is returned and completed satisfactorily, the student receives his or her recess privileges again. There are different sheets with different topics. This method lightens my time commitment in discipline, informs parents, and provides biblical direction, while the students learn to take responsibility for their actions.

The following is a Character Builder sheet for stewardship. Space is given for students to answer the questions and also for the parents to sign.

Stewardship

Answer the following questions. Write neatly and in complete sentences. When you are finished, review this with your parent(s) and have them sign at the bottom:

1. What was the problem?
2. How could you have avoided the problem?
3. How can you solve the problem?
4. Look up (state number) of the following passages in the Bible. Tell what each of them says about stewardship: Prov. 10:4, Prov. 19:15, Col. 3:23, Prov. 13:4, Prov. 12:24, Prov. 21:5, 2 Thess. 3:10, 1 Thess. 5:12, Prov. 13:4, Prov. 26:15, Prov. 12:27.
5. How can I help you win this struggle?

I have separate Character Builder sheets for various qualities of character: Love, Respect, Obedience, Speaking Appropriately, Self-Control, Honesty.

Jeff Poppema, Community Christian School, 1300 19th Ave. S.W., Willmar, MN 56201. Phone: 612-235-0592

Kathy Eggimann, a seventh grade teacher also at Community Christian School, has developed supplementary material for the CSI health curriculum. The material is too lengthy to describe here, but she can be contacted at Community Christian School in Willmar, Minnesota (same address and telephone as above).

Jim Rauwerda, Byron Center Christian School, Byron Center, Michigan

Stock Sales

I divide my American history class in half. Each group of ten to fifteen must form a company and give it a name. They print stock certificates and sell them—yes, for real money. For example, often they will print fifty shares and sell them for one dollar each. With the money, they buy candy (or anything else) and sell it in the halls at break to the younger students—again, for real money. They must use some of their money to pay a tax on their profits, to advertise their product, and to meet other expenses. Shareholders are able to profit by cashing in their stocks, and members of each company divide the rest of the money. There is no competition since each company sells on a different day, but there is profit, which the students like very much. I've never had a group lose money, and the project provides great material for a discussion of economics and America's free enterprise system.

Retirement Home Visit

On a field trip to a retirement home, my American history students interview residents about the Great Depression, any wars they remember (such as World War II or the Korean War), and life in the 1950s.

Historical Fiction

My American history students are given a picture of a child immigrant. They must imagine and write their immigrant's "story"—an example of historical fiction. The details in their stories reflect what they've learned about immigrants and

Appendix

immigration in class and through outside reading. The pictures and stories are displayed on a bulletin board.

Theme Week

Theme Week is an event for the entire middle school. Each year the teachers choose a theme (the 1960s, the West, the Middle Ages, Space) and schedule field trips, speakers, multi-grade "classes," and schoolwide activities that center around that theme. This year, for example, the theme is Space, and a number of speakers will be coming. We will visit the planetarium, and we hope to have a "night class" in which Grand Rapids' amateur astronomers will set up telescopes in the parking lot and show students the constellations.

Jim Rauwerda, Byron Center Christian School, 8840 Byron Center Ave. SW, Byron Center, MI 49315

Reaching and Teaching Young Adolescents

Reaching and Teaching Young Adolescents